Caroline Crane Marsh

Wolfe of the Knoll

And Other Poems

Caroline Crane Marsh

Wolfe of the Knoll
And Other Poems

ISBN/EAN: 9783744653077

Printed in Europe, USA, Canada, Australia, Japan

Cover: Foto ©Thomas Meinert / pixelio.de

More available books at **www.hansebooks.com**

WOLFE OF THE KNOLL,

AND OTHER POEMS.

BY

MRS. GEORGE P. MARSH.

NEW YORK:
CHARLES SCRIBNER, GRAND STREET.
LONDON:
SAMPSON LOW, SON & COMPANY.
1860.

ENTERED, according to Act of Congress, in the year 1859, by
CHARLES SCRIBNER,
In the Clerk's Office of the District Court of the United States for the Southern District of New York.

CONTENTS.

	PAGE
WOLFE OF THE KNOLL,	13
NIÖRTHR AND SKATHI,	229
A FABLE,	236
THE MAID OF THE MERRY HEART,	238
A LAY OF THE DANUBE:	
I. The Wissehrad,	240
II. The Magyar Maid,	242
DANIEL, THE CISTERCIAN,	248
THE FOUNTAIN OF THE POOR,	251
THE WATER OF EL ARBAÏN,	256
AXEL (from the Swedish of Tegnér),	261
SONG OF THE LAPLAND LOVER (from the Swedish of Franzén),	308
THE MOSS-ROSE (from the German of Helmine von Chezy),	311
THE GLOW-WORM (from the German of Helmine von Chezy),	314
A GODLIE HYMNE (from the German of Zuinglius),	316
TO ———,	324

WOLFE OF THE KNOLL.

INTRODUCTION.

The scene of the following poem is laid alternately on the island of Amrum near the coast of the duchy of Schleswig-Holstein, and in the city of Tunis and the territory of that Beylik. In the descriptions of the island and of the manners of its inhabitants, are embraced not only the characteristic features of Amrum itself, but those belonging to the Halligs, or low tide-washed islands of the same shallow waters, and they have been drawn principally from J. G. Kohl's "*Marschen und Inseln der Herzogthümer Schleswig und Holstein,*" and from a tale by Biernatzki.

The singular geography of the Frisian country, and the strange life of its people, seem to have made a powerful impression on Tacitus and the elder Pliny. The latter gives, in Book xvi., chap. i. of his "*Natural History,*" a lively description of the scene of this part of our story, which, in the words of Kohl, "is as faithful and striking, as if, like me, he had himself sailed over from Wyk to Oland with Skipper Jilke Junk Jürgens." For Holland's translation of the passage the reader is referred to the Appendix I.

Tacitus, speaking of Germany generally, argues that the

people must have been indigenous, because no man would ever leave Asia, Africa or Italy, and brave the horrors of the deep, to become a resident of so desolate and wretched a region. It appears, both from his testimony and from other sources, that the Frisians of the coast and the islands have, from the earliest ages, been remarkable for their courage and independence. For an amusing version of the story of the two ambassadors, whose appearance in the theatre at Rome is commemorated by TACITUS, Annal. 13, 54, the reader is again referred to the Appendix II.

The pictures of the Sahara, and of the wild tribes who traverse it, are drawn partly from the writer's personal observation of desert-life and scenery, and partly from authorities which will be given hereafter.

The leading incidents of the story are taken from a tradition contained in the first chapter of the second volume of KOHL's work, and the name of the poem is from the same source.

It may be unnecessary to say, that the narrative is intended to serve merely as a thread to connect the strong contrasts of life and nature offered by the peculiar regions that have been selected for description.

WOLFE OF THE KNOLL.

CANTO I.

AMROOM.

Come, ye that are weary of heart, with me
To a far-off isle in a lonely sea!
It lies, not glowing 'neath tropical skies,
Cradled in waters of amethyst dyes;
No vine-wreaths are there, no feathery palms,
No blossoms are filling the air with balms,
No forests are waving, no stately trees—
Grand organs played by the tune-loving breeze—
Not even a coppice where summer birds throng
Dazzling with plumage or thrilling with song;
No stream leapeth wild from the mountain-side,

'Neath cavernous rocks for a moment to hide,
Then calmly through winding valleys to glide.
No lake nestles there, with its fairy skiffs,
Half silvered by moonlight, half shaded by cliffs.
Our desolate choice hath no charms like these,
Sad hearts to comfort, or glad ones to please.
The sea casteth pearls on Araby's strand,
Shells, corals, and sea-moss, and ruby sand;
And emerald, scarlet, and gold fish there
Flash through his waters transparent as air.
His wavelets are laughing all night on that shore,
Tossing their jewels at touch of the oar.*
But angry and hoarse is the voice of the tide,
As he lashes our island's trembling side,
And rolls up the ooze from his slimy bed,
The pale thin meadows to overspread,
Then leaves, as he slowly sinketh back,
The muscle, the crab, and the ray in his track.

---

* The brilliant flashes of phosphoric light, seen when the waves dash upon the reefs, or are broken by the oar or otherwise, are called by the Arabs "the jewels of the deep."

Else few are the gifts that he bringeth the while;
He weareth at best but a mocking smile,
Like a foe confessed, who knoweth his power,
And his victim's weakness, yet bides the hour.*

On the North Sea's icy and heaving breast
The islet of AMROOM finds doubtful rest,
Above the wild waters scarce holdeth its place,
And bleak are the winds that sweep o'er its face
All bare to the blast, for shelter is none,
Save what the billows in scorn have upthrown—
The downs low and broken along the strand,
'Gainst the North Sea a rampart of shifting sand.
'Twould seem that King Ægir,† in merry mood,
Would teach us to fetter his own wild flood.

---

* One is constantly reminded by the figurative language of the people that the whole coast is at war with the sea. They always speak of the west wind and the ocean as "the enemy;" of the downs and dykes as "the defences and intrenchments against the enemy;" of the outer tier of islands as "the vanguard," and of the inner as "the rear-guard."

† In the Scandinavian mythology Ægir is a sea-god, who personifies the destructive, as Njörd does the beneficent powers of the ocean.

But man may not trust to his treacherous art—
One stroke, in his wrath, and those hills shall part!
The rest of the island, level and low,
The turbulent tide doth oft overflow,
Nor is thus contented; but day by day
Doth he crumble that dwindling sod away,
And foot by foot it is narrowing fast;
All will be melted in ocean at last.

But who are the dwellers on this lone spot
By nature herself disowned and forgot,
That here we should linger in such a waste,
Unblest as the fancy of poet e'er traced!
Why seek we not, rather, some coralline isle
Of seas Pacific, to feast for awhile
On flowers that would seem to our wondering eyes
To have dropped from the fields of Paradise—
On fruits that a flavor as rich might boast
As the pride of Ulysses' royal host—
Where beauty, as soft as the Latmian dreams

Of England's slain poet, forever beams—
Where mermaids hollow their sparkling caves
In the crystal rocks that the cool tide laves,
And blow sweet airs through their pearly shells
Till wide o'er the island the harmony swells?
Ah! our brother man—so fallen, so low!
With an aching heart we should turn and go!
Then choose for our dreaming this desert sod,
With a truth-loving folk, that feareth God!

Through fiery haze descends the sun,
And throws across the waters dun
A slender band of ruddy stain
So bright it seems the golden chain,
That binds earth to his glorious sphere,
Is visibly extended here,
And that the dancing waves may break
The flashing links they rudely shake.
Tranquilly doth our islet sleep,
This eventide, upon the deep.

O'er its bare face the slant rays pass
And gild it with a tender glow,
Leaving no image on the grass,
Of rocky crag or greenwood bough;
The crescent line of downs alone
Hath eastward a broad shadow thrown,
And the poor cotter's lowly roof,
From angry spring-tides held aloof
By the turfed mound his hands have reared*
Above the reach of foe so feared,
In lengthening lines fantastic drawn,
Lies pictured on the sea-washed lawn;
While flocks, slow drawing toward each thatch,
Still eager, their scant pasture snatch.
His homeward path the peasant treads,
His children gather at his knee,
Their slender board the mother spreads—
Here all is peace and poverty.

---

* The inhabitants of these tide-islands are obliged to erect their humble dwellings on artificial mounds raised above the reach of high-water.

AMROOM.

Without, no sound but the low dash
Of tidal wave, the cry or plash
Of the wild sea-bird, glancing bright
As starry meteor in its flight.
No children on that strand are seen
Grouped merrily in noisy play,
No muser marks with thoughtful mien
The dying splendors of the day,
No stranger-eyes with wonder view
A scene so lonely and so new.

But on yon knoll an old man stands
With furrowed cheeks and toil-worn hands;
His long, loose hair is bleached as hoar
As the bright foam that wreathes the shore;
His form, erect in youthful prime,
Bends 'neath the gathered griefs of time;
Yet on that calm, sad brow is laid
Of wrong, revenge, remorse, no shade;
Though deeply traced are sorrow's lines,

The light of faith still clearly shines.
Most like a child who, while it grieves,
Still in a father's love believes,
The old man seems; and as the child,
To free its sight, doth push away
The ringlets from its forehead mild,
So throws he back his locks of gray,
Then searches long and eagerly
The horizon of that turbid sea.
With footstep hushed and pitying eye
The shepherds silent pass him by,
And every child is taught to show
Meet reverence for that head of snow.

Nor first this eve upon that hill
The aged WOLFE doth watch, but still,
Day after day, his stooping form
May there be seen, in calm and storm,
His eye turned ever to the sea,
North, west, and south, untiringly.

No rising sun but finds him there,
Nor misses him the evening star,
And the pale moon doth nightly shed
Her cold light on his frosted head.
First when the pall of darkest night
Hath fallen, the old man leaves the height.
What doth he there? Hath fancy wrought
Within his brain some strange misthought?
Is it some vision that he sees,
A phantom-child of mist and breeze?
Ah, no! he waiteth for his boy,
The island's pride, his heart's last joy!

Young MELLEFF was as brave as good,
A bolder lad ne'er stemmed the flood.
None ventured with a foot so free
To dare the treacherous tide as he.
When winds and waves the islet shook,
His arm secured the trembling flock.
Nor less his manly heart was shown

In others' need, than in his own,
And oft admiring neighbors told,
How the boy's courage saved their fold.
But long ago this only son
A shepherd's for a sailor's life
Exchanged, and even years have flown,
Since hope and fear, in ceaseless strife,
Within the parent's heart have dwelt—
Ye know that grief who such have felt!
Once, only, tidings had been brought,
Tidings with hope and comfort fraught;
The youth ' was soon to sail for home,
No more from the dear sod to roam,
Truth, charity, and peace were there,
The world without was cold and drear.'
But he comes not—the mother sleeps,
Weary with watching, in the grave,
Yet still the lonely father keeps
His eye upon the distant wave;

He there may chance a ship to see,
And in that ship his child may be!

Old HELDA, widowed, poor and weak,
Was wandering on that beach, to seek
For sticks to light her evening fire,
When she beheld the anxious sire
Again on the accustomed hill.
"Thank God!" she cried, "it was His will
To grant a lot less hard to me,
Than this—year after year to be
Mocked by vain hopes unceasingly.
Better to know my children rest
With God, and Christ, and angels blest,
And to live calm in the meek trust
To join them when this frame is dust!"
Once more upon the down she cast
Her eyes, but night was gathering fast;
"God help him!" then her old lips pray,
And, with a sigh, she turns away.

CANTO II.

TUNIS-THE-WHITE.

Where lingers the son of the cloudy North!
Hath he forgotten the home of his birth?
Careth he not that his sire hath grown gray
With watching and praying by night and by day?
As soon shall a mother forget her child
As the wandering boy his islet wild,
And thoughts of the eyes that wake and weep
For him, hold his own weary lids from sleep.
Thou, thou dost keep him, O marvellous land
Of the sourceless river, the boundless sand!
Visions of Amroom—home yearnings are vain!
Fast, fast is he bound by the captive's chain.

TUNIS-THE-WHITE.

On Tunis bright the sunbeams fall,
Where, girded by her double wall,
She sits a queen, upon whose brow
A thousand flashing crescents glow,
Forming a diadem to vie
With Maia's crown that flames on high.
Goodly, without, her vesture shows—
Scarce purer white the mountain-snows.
Who saw her thus, in royal state,
Kissed by the bounding wave so free,
Even lovely Venice might forget,
And hail her there, 'Bride of the Sea!'
Fair are her minarets and towers,
Her rosy gardens, viny bowers;
Her fountains gush as clear and cold
As ever naiad's source of old,
And softer murmurs than they shed
Rose not from fond Alpheus' bed,
When Arethusa stooped to lave
Her tender limbs in his bright wave.

Her marts are heaped with merchandise,
Such as the gorgeous East supplies;
Buyers and sellers throng her gates,
And at her feet a navy waits.

But now half-silent are her streets,
So fearfully the noontide beats
On the white arches, whose fierce glare
Scorches the eye; the burning air
Is choked with sand the Khamseen * brings
Upon its swift and dreadful wings.
Within their halls the rich repose,
Their vacant shops the salesmen close.
But the poor hammal † bendeth still
Beneath his load; the sakkas ‡ fill

---

* Khamseen—from khamsoon, fifty—is the name usually given to a strong south wind which blows throughout northern Africa, and especially in the valley of the Nile, at intervals through a period of about fifty days in the months of April, May, and June.

† Hammal, the Arabic word for porter; a very important class of laborers in Oriental cities, where wheel-carriages are not used.

‡ Sakka, a water-carrier. See Appendix III.

Their water-skins afresh, while some
Offer free draughts to all who come,
In name of the good Moslem soul
Whose bounty fills the brimming bowl.
The patient ass, that none will spare,
His crushing burden still must bear
Through the close lanes, while curses sore
The jostled passers on him pour.
These may not choose, they may not rest;
Though faint with heat, with hunger pressed,
The poor, the brute, must toil or feel
From want or violence sharper ill.

Fanned by his slaves, the lordly Bey
On Persian mats soft dreaming lay.
Spacious the court and cool the air,
A thousand jets were playing there,
Breathing a low and hushing sound
More calm than silence; all around
Choice flowers their fairest bloom were spreading,

Through marble halls their perfume shedding;
And panting birds were flocking there,
The freshness, without fear, to share;
For well the happy warblers know
The Prophet's follower ne'er their foe.
But not a human voice was heard,
And not a human footstep stirred.
Silent as stone, each watchful slave
Moved but the ostrich plume to wave;
So deep a stillness must be kept,
To guard the rest of him that slept!

But hark! there is a cry without!
' Allah is great!' the faithful shout.
The voice of triumph in the street
Starts AALI from his slumber sweet.
He sends a slave the cause to learn—
'Tis for the corsair's safe return;
New prizes in the harbor ride
To swell Tunisia's wealth and pride.

The victors towards the Casbah* press,

Cheered by the joyful populace.

Only last moon, like birds of prey,

On rapid wing they swept away,

And, as if gifted with the same

Mysterious sense that guideth them

Unfailing where their victim lies,

Sudden as bolt from the clear skies,

They lighted on the Franks too near

A Christian shore to dream of fear.

Their chieftain boasts that he is come

Of the great line of Khair-ed-deen,†

---

* The Casbah is a castellated fortress at Tunis, adjacent to which is the palace of the Bey, Dar el Bey, and it gives name to a public square called the "Square of the Casbah."

† Khair-ed-deen, *the Excellence of the Religion*, [*of Islam*,] generally known to Europeans by the name of Barbarossa, was a native of Mytilene, and of Moslem birth and education, as appears by his own autobiography, and not a renegade as he has usually been represented. He was the Nelson of the Ottoman marine in the sixteenth century, and conquered for the Porte the regencies of Algiers and Tunis. No Turkish maritime commander has ever made himself so formidable to the Franks, and the whole coast of Spain and Italy was in a perpetual state of alarm while he was at the head of the Ottoman navy.

The terror once of Christendom,
That ne'er a bolder foe hath seen;
And many a deed of blood and fire
Have proved him worthy of a sire,
Who made dread Barbarossa's name
The Paynim's pride, the Christian's shame.
Yet was not MURAD merciless;
Nor poor nor stranger would oppress;
Ne'er lacked, beneath his roof, the 'guest
Of God invited'* food or rest.
Five times a day with zeal he prayed
Toward Mecca bowed his shaven head,
Kept fitting fast, and freely gave
Whene'er the poor an alms might crave.
Such duties did he ne'er forget.
Had not the Prophet clearly set
These precepts above every other—

---

* 'The invited of God' is the name given to a stranger who asks hospitality. When a traveller approaches an encampment, he cries, "O master of the tent! Lo, a guest invited of God!" and seldom fails to receive the attention and the comforts which his wants require. For the traditional sayings of the Prophet on this subject, see Appendix IV.

Worship to God, love to his brother?
But Christians—was it not as plain
That they were infidels, not men,
Not brothers—rather dogs, indeed!
Have we not heard as strange a creed?
When late an iron despot raised
His arm, to crush a monarch praised
Of all, for mild and liberal laws,
A friend to every generous cause,
Whose empire's gates are open flung
To every faith and every tongue,
From our free land a chorus burst
To cheer the tyrant's deed accursed.
' A Christian this, a Moslem he,
Can need of further witness be?'
Vain man! thus ever, to thy shame,
Cheating or cheated with a name!
Think'st thou that Paul would sooner set
Mary o'er Christ than Mahomet?

But now too long the corsair waits
For audience at the palace-gates.
Behold him then before the Bey,
Greeting, as Moslem subject may,
His haughty lord, who bids him tell
How he hath spoiled the infidel.
Briefly showed Murad, as was meet,
That he had seized a merchant-fleet
Near Sicily's frequented coast—
' Complete the triumph that we boast,
And rich the booty that we bear,
Well worthy for a prince to share.
The slaves are countless—men and boys—
They stand without, and wait thy choice.'

" Allah is great, and thou art brave,"
Replied the Bey, and signal gave
That, score by score, the Christians should
Be brought before him; as they stood,
His keen eye saw, at one quick glance,

Of a large ransom what the chance,
And thus he chose—an eighth of all
By law doth to the pacha fall.

But who shall paint the captives' woe—
Anguish that words are vain to show!
Wouldst thou thy curious fancy teach,
The means are not beyond thy reach.
Nor need imperial Catharine rise
To aid the artist's hard emprise.
A Christian land doth furnish forth
The spectacle to the whole earth,
With truth more awful to the soul
Than to the ear the thunder-roll,
When to the skies the dreadful blast
The frigate's blazing fragments cast,
Shadowing to Hackert's wondering sight
The horrors of the Tchesmian fight.*

* To enable Hackert to paint more truthfully the great naval victory won by the Russian fleet over the Turkish at Tchesme in 1770, Admiral Orloff, by order of the empress, blew up a Russian frigate off Leghorn.

Enough, 'twas sad those Franks to see
Fettered before the Osmanli.
Shame and despair reigned in each face,
And left for pride but little place.
Yet Aali spake no word of scorn;
His was a soul too nobly born
To mock the grief of that sad throng,
Though conscience charged him not with wrong.
Nor looked he there a tyrant fierce,
With breast that pity could not pierce,
Nor seemed more careless of distress
Than those who gentler faith profess.
A little girl upon his knee
Was leaning lovingly and free;
Too tender yet her age to learn
Those lessons of submission stern,
And reverence, that the law requires,
Of Moslem children toward their sires;
Nor veil nor lattice yet control
The freedom of her joyous soul.

See! the proud pacha's hand is laid
As fondly on his daughter's head
As ever Christian father mild
Hath rested his upon his child.
And ne'er did opening flower disclose,
Since Chaucer saw his budding rose
So rich in beauty and perfume,
The promise of a fairer bloom,
Than even the careless eye must trace
In FATMEH's childish form and face.
Her large black eye with its clear ray
Spoke of near kinship to the Bey,
Yet tempered were its rising flashes
By the long drooping silken lashes,
That o'er those orbs transparent hung,
And down their trembling shadows flung,
Like willow-boughs that fringe a lake,
And its pure sheen less dazzling make.
The ebon arches o'er them bent
Were true as Giotto's hand could paint.

In her dark, heavy tresses shone
A burnished light, as if the sun
Had softly kissed the glossy hair,
And left his golden radiance there;
Proving that gleam, so strange inwrought
In the deep twilight of her braids,
From a Circassian mother caught,
With curls as bright as Saxon maids.
But she is gone; the fairy child,
Half passionate, half angel-mild,
No kin doth know, save him who now
So gently smooths her snowy brow.
And next an ancient nurse she loves,
And then her song-birds, flowers and doves.
At first she little marks the crowd
Of captives chained and sorrow-bowed,
(For she was wont from infancy
The witness of such scenes to be,)
And with impatience ill-repressed,
Waits for the troop to be dismissed,

That she may fill the pacha's ear
With prattle fathers love to hear.
But as the Bey, with rapid sign,
Drew one by one from the sad line
For his own thrall, a look she cast
Curious, scarce pitying, as they passed,
Until her full dilating gaze
A sudden earnestness betrays;
For lo, a youth with sunny locks,
And eyes whose humid azure mocks
The dewy violet's purest shade,
Attracts the wondering little maid.
Of bearing bold, of stature high,
With sword-cuts fresh on brow and breast,
Though sorrow dimmed his dreamy eye,
His manly lip was firm comprest.
Oft from old GERDA had she heard,—
And much the tale her fancy stirred,—
That in the cold and distant North,
Land of her foster-mother's birth,

Were men as any maiden fair,
With ruddy cheeks and golden hair,
And eyes whose depths of cloudless blue
Might rival Afric's sky in hue,
Yet never form of grander mould
Than theirs, nor heart more true and bold.
No sooner did her quick eye fall
Upon the prisoner fair and tall,
Than straight she thinks of Gerda's home,
And questions if he thence doth come,
Nor rests, till with sweet childhood's art,
She has learned all they can impart.
'The Christian youth was from the North,
Melleff his name;' she rushes forth
To tell her nurse, with thoughtless joy,
Of the strange blue-eyed captive boy.

CANTO III.

THE TIDINGS.

On Amroom are sunshine and summer to-day;
  And it seems less lone and drear;
The islanders gather in heaps their hay,
  Their hope for the coming year.

And father and mother and youth and maid,
  All join in the common toil;
Earnest their work and the words that are said,—
  Mirth flies from so rude a soil.

And ever a shadow yet graver still
  O'er each laborer's face doth pass,
As he sendeth a glance toward yonder hill
  Where shivers the tufted grass.

There, seemingly heedless of all around,
    With the sea-damps on his cheek,
Stands Wolfe—lo, he turns toward the new-mown ground,
    And beckons as he would speak!

"To-morrow's the sabbath, the day of rest,"
    Said the old man grave and mild,
"Your hay, if with sunshine again we're blest,
    Will make as it lieth piled.

"Ye may sleep to-night without care or fear;
    I will watch the wind and tide;
Should they threaten your harvest, ye shall hear
    My warning echo wide."

The labor is ended, and one by one
    They go to their quiet homes;
From the snowy flocks each calleth his own,
    Ere the misty darkness comes.

Then climbing the mound that lifteth their cot
    From the low and tide-washed sward,
At peace with themselves, and blessing their lot,
    They draw round the evening board.

Though coarse the loaf that is broken here,
    And it formeth, day by day,
With curds from the flock, their only cheer
    Yet murmur nor want know they.

Now meekly, but clear, from each lowly shed
    Ascendeth the hymn, and the prayer;
The simple rite done, and the 'good-night' said,
    The household to rest doth repair.

And well may they slumber, so deep the repose;
    For there is nor sight nor sound,
Save the moon above, that so ruddy rose,
    And the sea low moaning round.

But while those evening hymns were sent
Heavenward, one voice of deep lament
And supplication from that sod
Wailed upward to the throne of God.
WOLFE OF THE KNOLL upon the shore,
With searching eye, was seen no more;
No more upon the fitful breeze
His locks of silver rose and fell,
Restless as on those heaving seas
The crested billows sink and swell.
The promised watchman of the night,
That late stood calm on yonder height,
Now on his lowly pallet lies
With breaking heart and burning eyes.
This eve the fatal tidings gave
That Melleff was the heathen's slave.
The pastor, first to learn, must show
The hapless father all his woe.

Dread task! and now in vain he tries
To assuage that grief—the old man cries:
" Nay, leave me here with God alone,
Till I can say, ' His will be done ! ' "

The dawn is cloudless, the summer-sun shines
   Again on the grateful isle;
They may leave their hay till the day declines,
   To worship their God, the while.

And early they gather, with willing feet,
   At their humble place of prayer;
In simple attire, and with reverence meet,
   The old and the young are there.

The service is read, and the preacher takes
   The word that they wait to hear—
Hark! whence is the threatening sound that breaks
   From without on his startled ear?

"My children, God sendeth the flood! away,
    And secure your winter store!
His blessing be with you—we'll meet to pray
    Again when our work is o'er."

They fly to the meadows; the tide swells fast,
    But something there's time to save!
The share of their faithful pastor, at least,
    They'll snatch from the greedy wave.

In vain he urgeth to care for their own,
    The strength of his well-tried arm,—
For no! they will toil in his field alone,
    Till its math is safe from harm.

Must the rest be lost? strain every nerve,
    For the hungry wave is nigh!
Brief is the moment, yet still it may serve—
    How from heap to heap they fly!

And higher, still higher, upon the land
    Doth the angry ocean chafe—
With a smile of triumph the islanders stand,
    Their precious harvest is safe!

O'er the meadows a briny sea doth flow,
    But baffled, its tides decrease;
And pastor and people once more may go
    To the house of God in peace.

Again they are taught from his holy word,
    Again they praise and they pray,
And with glowing hearts do they bless the Lord
    For the mercies of the day.

But last, and earnester still, are the prayers
    That they for the father pour—
That God would remember his hoary hairs,
    And his captive child restore!*

---

* Although the people are very devout, they allow themselves to be interrupted even in divine service by the approach of a tide which threatens

The holy sabbath rites are o'er,
And through the consecrated door,
With voices hushed, the shepherds pour.

The weary pastor, only, turns
Not homeward yet; his spirit yearns
To soothe the wretched father reft
Of the last hope that time had left.

Still in the narrow porch he stands,
His eye o'ersweeps the ebb-land wide,
Then of the westering sun demands
How soon returns the treacherous tide.

Another hour—his wary foot

---

their hay-crop, and they then rush to the fields in their Sunday garments. A Hallig preacher told me he had once just began his sermon, when he observed a movement in the congregation. One of the people soon came up the pulpit steps, and, pulling him by the cassock, whispered, "Pastor, the water is coming!" He therefore dismissed the congregation, requesting them to return to the church after the work was ended, and went with them to the meadows. In about three hours they secured their hay, and met again at the church, to thank God for the saving of their only source of income.

In the island of Helgoland, the arrival of the snipes authorizes the interruption of worship. When the flocks alight, no time must be lost; and if the watchman calls at the church door, "Herr, pastor, de snipp is do!" "Pastor, the snipes are here!" the clergyman breaks off the service.—*Kohl Ins. u. Marsch.* I. 325.

THE TIDINGS.

May he not trust upon the beach,
That leads so shortly to the cot
His eager heart makes haste to reach?
He'll swiftly cross the waves' dark track,
No threatening sea-mists warn him back.

The doubtful soil he now doth tread,
So late the refluent ocean's bed.
What change was here! an hour before,
No sound except the tide's deep roar,
No life save what its bosom bore.
Now man's weak step is tracking free
The footprints of the mighty sea!
A thousand channels, pearled with foam,
Are rippling toward their briny home;
And countless forms of life, sea-born,
Left by their parent wave forlorn,
Lie struggling on the slimy strand,
Foes gathering fast on every hand.
With a sharp cry the swooping gull

Drops on his prey; in the still pool
Dips the sea-swallow swift and light,
Then nestward takes his happy flight.
The rain-bird, pressed with hunger fell,
Tears the poor muscle from its shell,
And still new flocks are hurrying there,
The transitory spoil to share.
Far to the west, the eye may mark
Where, leaning low upon its side,
Lieth the fisher's helpless bark,
And passive waits the coming tide.*

Full oft the zealous man of God
That wild and wasting shore has trod,
And well he knows each changing phase
That home of poverty displays.
Yet doth it seem as strange to-night,
As on the well-remembered day,
When first before his straining sight

---

* Staring, De Bodem van Nederland, I. 231, gives a very picturesque description of the flats at low-tide.

Its dreamlike desolation lay.

What years of toil and sacrifice

Between him and that moment rise! *

Yet time that moment doth defy,

A fragment of eternity.

As then, he sees the eager crowd,

Half hidden by a misty shroud,

In costume quaint, press to the beach ;

Once more the friendly hand they reach,

Once more, with childlike speech and smile,

They bid him welcome to their isle.

He sees his meek, young wife, again

Covered with changeful blushes, when

They hail her by the tender name

Of 'mother,' † and her blessing claim.

Now to the cottage, garnished fair

For the new pastor, they prepare

---

* For an account of the arrival of a Hallig preacher in his parish, see Appendix V.

† The pastor's wife is always called mother, and they say to her, " We have come to invite mother to our christening, if mother has no objection."

His little household store to bear,
And now his willing feet they guide
To the near church, their only pride.
Once more, from that same chapel mound,
He marks the dreary prospect round,
With anxious heart and wondering eye.
Here must he live—perhaps must die.

But o'er his thoughts thus backward cast,
Behold, a sudden change hath past,
For, by the law mysterious led
That links extremes, his fancy flies
From the low flats around him spread,
To lands where mountains pierce the skies.
The everlasting Alps she shows
Shaking from their o'erburdened brows
The crushing avalanche, that falls
In thunder down their rocky walls.
She pointeth from the idle boat
To the bold hunter, whose winged foot
Pursues the chamois' headlong flight,

O'er rock and rift, from height to height.
The tangled sea-grass, coarse and dank,
Is lost in flowery meadows bright;
No more a gray horizon blank,
But fringing forests, bound his sight.
The turbid channel's bitter stream
Hath vanished in that happy dream,
And lo, before the wanderer's soul
Sweet floods of living crystal roll,
And laughing cataracts madly leap;
Girt with a rainbow, down the steep,
From crag to crag—such as with joy
To fulness blessed him, when a boy.—
That boyhood, with its dear delights,
The days half labor and half play,
The fireside full that crowned the nights—
The starting tear he cannot stay,
So plain he sees the loving forms
That blessed him, when he turned away
To seek this cheerless isle of storms.

Hark! dost not hear the hoarse wave break
Upon the shore? wake, dreamer, wake!
He starts, as from a heavy sleep;
He sees the broadening channels deep
Weaving full fast their watery net
Around his thoughtless, lagging feet.
Then shot an icy shudder through
His frame—' wife, children, leave them so,
Alone upon this wretched sod!
Can this be, then, thy will, O God?'
A moment brief, with horror fraught,
Flashed by, then came a calmer thought;
' He that hath made can still sustain,
Nor needs thy aid, O mortal vain!'
His heart grows still, the dread is past,
Fear's palsying fetters broken through;
Toward the near cot he boundeth fast,
And fast the hissing waves pursue.
In vain—they cannot reach him now!
High on the cottage-mound he stands,

Wipes the thick drops from his hot brow,

And lifts to Heaven his trembling hands.

Yet from his lips no sound there fell—

What words for such a moment meet,

When the whole heart doth upward swell,

In one full cloud of incense sweet!

One backward glance he shrinking cast

Upon the fearful peril past,*

Then, turning to the roof of thatch,

He slowly lifts the simple latch.

O, grief! whose heart is then so clean,

Whose hands in innocence so washed,

That he thy sacred form hath seen,

And stood before thee unabashed!

To thy great altar who dares bring,

For offering, an unholy thing!

---

* When the tide returns suddenly, persons walking on the flats during the ebb are exposed to be cut off from the islands and drowned. Distressing accidents of this kind are not unfrequent.

Only the soul's best gifts can meet
Acceptance at thine awful feet.

So felt the pastor, as he stood
Speechless beside the man of woe,
And grasped his withered hand, nor could
The sympathetic tear forego.
On those three friends of old he thought,
Whose seven days' silence better spake
Than all the empty words they brought,
Which did but keener anguish wake.
God's voice alone such sorrow hears;
Of man, it asks not truths, but tears.
He lifts a silent prayer on high—
Lo, suddenly the stricken sire
Looks up, his pale lips part, his eye
Doth burn, as with a prophet's fire,
And his full words swell, clear and strong,
As chorus of triumphal song.

"The Lord will surely visit him,
And bring back his captivity!
Yea, though these eyes with age are dim,
They shall this great salvation see!"

CANTO IV.

THE HAREEM.

Thank God, the lingering sun hath set at last!
    The daily task is o'er;
Another long, long day of exile past!
    Oh, that there were no more!

What though yon glorious western sky doth blaze
    With purple, gold, and green,
While the east trembles with those opal rays
    By northern eyes unseen!

What though from the transparent heavens so clear
    The stars are stooping low!
The greeting of their smile, that comes so near,
    Seems but to mock my woe.

THE HAREEM.

Ye northern skies, your light is gray and cold,
    But dearer far to me
Than all the splendors that I now behold
    In heaven, earth, air and sea!

Thou isle, where innocence and peace so long
    Have kept their holiest rest,
Forgive me that, a child, I did thee wrong,
    Asking a soil more blest!

Oft by some stinted shrub I pensive stood,
    And dreamed of giant trees
That proudly soared aloft, and swung abroad
    Their branches to the breeze.

Now o'er my head a leafy roof doth rise
    For sinless Eden meet,
Dropping its golden fruit as from the skies,
    In clusters at my feet.

But one poor bush that decks our cottage-mound,
    My mother's constant care,
Than all these palms with grace and beauty crowned,
    Were to my eye more fair.

Here brightly blooming flowers of countless dyes
    Wide gardens gayly paint;
Sadly I view them with unjoying eyes,
    Till with their perfume faint.

Oh, give me but for these the pale wild rose
    Found once in many a day
Among our downs, in some deep fold hid close,
    Where childhood loved to stray.

Cease, cease thy mournful plaint, O nightingale,
    Singing in yonder tree!
Not half so dear thy song as the familiar wail
    Of my own native sea.

Ye sparkling fountains, that with patient flow
    Feed all these shining rills,
Your ceaseless murmur, melancholy, low,
    My soul with anguish fills.

For in your voice I hear the unending moan
    Of father, mother mild,
Who now sit broken-hearted and alone,
    Despairing for their child.

O God! and must I never more behold
    My blessed island home!
Ne'er comfort more my parents now grown old
    With waiting till I come!

Last night methought my mother softly pressed
    Her hand upon my head;
She looked not sad, but on her lips did rest
    The smile worn by the dead.

O mother, mother, if thou dost indeed
   Stand by the throne of God,
From thy poor captive child, with Him, oh, plead,
   That He will take life's load!

Such were the thoughts that shook the breast
Of Melleff as he sat at rest,
Leaning against a stately palm
In the soft twilight's hallowed calm.
Within the garden he had toiled
All day, and now from work assoiled,
His whole soul flies to the far north,
To the dear sod that gave him birth.
His heart no hope of ransom cheers,
Full well he knows if parents' tears
Could pay the price, he soon were free.
But ah, their fatal poverty!

Daughter of wealth! a moment stay,
Ere to the dance thou haste away!

One little stone that none would miss
From the bright band that clasps thy hair—
So many more are shining there—
Would lightly purchase all the bliss
Of home and freedom for the boy,
And fill his father's house with joy.
Thou canst not give it? go thy way,
Tread fast the festive measure gay,
Yet oh! look to thy soul, ere He,
The prisoner's friend, in anger says,
"What thou didst not for one of these
That didst thou also not for me!"

From the proud Christian maiden's frown,
To misbelieving Fatmeh turn,
Who, from the lattice of her bower,
Observes the captive at this hour
So woful sad. "Gerda," she cries,
With look and tone that speak surprise,
"Why doth the Christian slave still weep?

Doth Mustapha, then, fail to keep
My father's oft enjoined behest,
That he should lack nor food nor rest?
Thou, too, when first the tale I told
Of Melleff and his hair of gold,
And thou didst go to prove my word,
With pity deep thy heart seemed stirred,
Nor from thy questions couldst thou leave;
Wherefore now suffer him to grieve?"

Not southern night, descending fast,
Could shade so dark and sudden cast
As o'er old Gerda's features passed—
Then with a sigh, she answered grave,
"Tears are the pastime of the slave!"

Young Fatmeh on her face still gazed,
With questioning eye and thought amazed.
"Do all slaves weep?" at length she cried;
"Not all"—the aged nurse replied,

"For some so long have worn the chain,
And sighed and wept and prayed in vain
For freedom, home and friends, that they
At last grown helpless, old and gray,
Dry joyfully each burning tear
To see the welcome grave so near."

The loving child her white arms flung
Around her nurse, and sobbing hung
On her old neck—"Say, Gerda, say,
Wouldst thou thy Fatmeh leave to-day
For home and friends so far away?"

"Child of my soul;* nay! for I've none.
Those that I loved are long forgone.
For all the North hath left, thy kiss,
My gentle child, I would not miss.
Of all my kin, a single heart
Still beats, and his a bitter part—

* A common Oriental epithet for an adopted child.

Or do I dream—so far from youth
And joy removed that dreams seem truth!
But such sad talking let us leave—
I promised thee a tale this eve."

"First from my hair these pearls unbind;
Thou say'st they are of wealth untold;
In the bazaars, couldst thou not find
One that for them would give me gold?"

"Thou hast thy mother's heart, fond child!
But speak no more, thy thought is wild.
List to me, rather, while I tell
What once an Arab maid befell."

"Nay, Gerda! but when late we passed
Where o'er the dead the aloe blooms,
While they beneath are sleeping fast—
Thou bad'st me mark, among the tombs,
One called the Christian lady's grave—
Now tell me, was she, too, a slave?"

THE TOMB OF THE CHRISTIAN PRINCESS.*

Long ago a noble lady dwelt in furthest Frankistan,
Of whose wondrous beauty tidings to remotest kingdoms ran;
Princes sued her royal father for his peerless daughter's hand
All in vain; the heart-free Ellen would not hear of marriage-band.

Once adown the garden walked she, fresh as Emily the bright
Seen, as chants the English rhymer, for the first time by Arcite;
And, like her, she plucked the roses, ere the sun had kissed away
Half the tears they shed in darkness for the absent lord of day.

---

* "The Tomb of the Christian Princess" is founded on a popular legend related by Prax in the *Revue de l' Orient*, for November, 1849.

Through the leafy aisles she floated, checking her own carol sweet,
While the morning hymn of nature rose so holy and complete;
And with such a smile she listened to each silvery-warbling bird,
Well it seemed she knew the meaning of the joyous notes she heard.

Now the outer wall she reaches, where so close the ivy clings,
But a garland scarcely snatches, ere a wicket open swings,
And a wretched troop, whose ankles bear the badge of heaviest woe,
Through the gateway roughly driven, to their daily task-work go.

All unseen the princess glided to the laurel's thickest shade,
On the turbaned captives gazing, half with wonder, half afraid.

Long she stands, as if enchanted—what has wrought that sudden spell?
In her eye are love and pity—is it Freya's miracle?*

Toward the palace then she turned her, but with languid foot and slow,
Minding now nor bird nor blossom, nor the bees that murmur low.
Some new thought her soul oppresses—how an hour hath changed that face!
Late there shone but careless pleasance, now miscase usurps its place.

Paler grew the gentle Ellen as the listless days rolled by,
Till the sad cheer of his daughter caught the troubled father's eye.
"Say, my child, what is't that grieves thee? where the gladsome step and smile,
With which thou wert wont to meet me, and my weary cares beguile?

---

* In the Scandinavian mythology, Freya is the goddess of love.

"Weep not for me, loving father, but so thickly comes my breath,
On my heart is such a pressure—it must be the hand of death!
Ere I go, one boon I pray thee, for the love thou bearest me,
For the sake of blessed Mary, set thy Moorish captives free!

"There is one they call Abdallah, royal is his step and eye—
Once he was the lord of Tunis, thou hast marked his bearing high,
And hast read in every gesture, he was Allah's slave, not thine—
When I lie beside my mother, give him from my hand this line."

And the sleep no sorrow breaketh then the lovely Ellen slept,
And the promise made her dying faithfully the father kept.
Soon the Arabs o'er the desert their fleet steeds are spurring fast,
High the yellow sand-clouds tossing, like the Simoom's smothering blast.

But before the prince Abdallah sought again his native land,
He had read the faint lines written by the passing maiden's hand.
" I have loved thee, noble stranger, but not better than my faith,
Lo the proof! I give thee freedom, and remain alone with death."

" Go thou to the tomb that holds me, from my hand a casket take,
And the jewels that thou findest—for the Christian princess' sake—
Buy with them the Christian captives that among thy people mourn;
Let them to their home and kindred and their fathers' God return!"

Straight he seeks the narrow chamber, sacred to fair Ellen's rest;
But what tongue may speak the wonder that affrays his startled breast!

There no Christian maid reposes, but a Moslem stiff and cold,
And a rosary wrought in Mecca fast the rigid fingers hold.*

As he stood amazed, bewildered, words that came not through the ear
To Abdallah's soul were whispered, "Take the chaplet, do not fear!"
Hastily the beads he snatches from the dead man's grasp, and flies,
On the pinions love had furnished, to the land of cloudless skies.

Soon he trod the streets of Tunis—but she knew her lord no more—
And to Zeitun's mosque he hastened, Allah's Oneness to adore.
As he stooped, the dusty sandal at the sacred door to leave,
Suddenly a hand ungentle seized him rudely by the sleeve.

* The Mohammedan uses a rosary in enumerating the repetitions occurring in his prayers. This rosary is composed of ninety-nine beads of wood, coral, or seeds, and is separated into three equal divisions by other beads of a peculiar form.

" Whence hast thou that chaplet, stranger? by the Prophet's head I swear,
'Tis my father's—tombs to rifle, misbeliever, dost thou dare?"
To the judge they drag Abdallah; straight the cadi gives command
To undo the vault sepulchral, and around the grave they stand,

But fall back in speechless terror—there, instead of Moslem shorn,
Lieth calm a smiling lady, fair as Houri heavenly born!
In her hand she held a casket, and her face shone like the day
For a moment when Abdallah gently took the trust away.

Long he listened hoping, praying, for some sound of coming breath,
But in vain—fair was the sleeper, yet she slept the sleep of death.

Soft he spread the turf above her, set the aloe on her breast—
'Had not Moonkir shown her favor, since he brought her there to rest?'

Then Abdallah did her bidding, and the Christian slaves dismissed;
Yet through life he left not weeping for the love he so had missed.
Twice two hundred times the date-tree proud hath donned her ruby crown,
Since beside the stranger-lady, old and worn he laid him down.

Still the story is remembered, and they say the princess lies
All unchanged in her first beauty, but secure from mortal eyes.
From the tomb a light proceedeth, that would blind with deadly pain,
Such as guards the Prophet's daughter from the gazer's glance profane.*

---

* A common superstition among the Mohammedans ascribes this miraculous power, not only to the tomb of the Prophet himself, but to that of "the Lady Fatmeh," his daughter, as well.

CANTO V.

THE RANSOM.

While thus his wretched child doth bear
The day's long toil, the night's unrest,
By strangers pitied and oppressed,
How doth it with the father fare?
We saw but lately, when his soul
Was dark with woe, God's angel roll
The stone of his dead hopes away,
And bid him rise to toil and pray!
And we, perchance, may find him still
Waiting upon his wonted hill.

Yes, there he stands, but not alone;
A silent group is gathered near,

In every face a sorrow shown,
In every eye a glistening tear,
And o'er the gray and rocking sea
They look as earnestly as he.
For on the horizon's distant verge
Beyond the crescent wall of foam—
Thrown up by the untiring surge—
That bends around their island-home,
Lighted by sunset's lustrous smile,
They still can see a snowy pile
Of canvas like a summer cloud; *
It bears the son beloved away
From the poor mother; old and bowed,
Who now with pallid lips doth pray;
It bears the husband from the arms
Of the lone wife here left to weep,
And from his first-born's baby-charms
Now on its mother's breast asleep;

* See Appendix VI.

It bears the lover from the maid,
To whom his only vows are given,
And from whose cheek the blood doth fade,
All backward to the full heart driven.

O, Poverty, thy rule is stern!
'Tis hard beneath thy frown to live,
And yet from thee thy children learn
The noblest lesson life can give,
The grace most glorious in the eyes
Of God and man—self-sacrifice!
When He, the Holy, came to show
The way our mortal feet should go,
If, one with Him, our souls would be
From torturing self forever free,
Through thy low vale His footsteps led,
On thy cold lap His sacred head
Was wont to find less certain rest
Than beast in lair, or bird in nest.

These women, clad in sable weeds,*
That stand upon the hillock here,
While o'er the wave yon vessel speeds
Freighted with all they hold most dear—
Think not they need our pitying tears!
Though want may force the loved away,
And they be left for weary years,
Yet they have learned to trust and pray.
Soon each will seek her quiet cot,
And there to God, on bended knee,
Unmurmuring at her lonely lot,
Commit the wanderer o'er the sea;
Then peaceful sleep, then patient rise
To labors fresh, fresh sacrifice.

Even now the last dark form is gone,
And Wolfe, the aged, stands alone.
More wasted still that stooping frame,
The pallor on his brow the same.

---

* The women of these islands always wear a mourning dress while their friends are at sea.

And yet since first we saw that eye
A clearer beam it sure hath caught;
It turns not now so dreamily,
As if uncertain what it sought!
But firmly, consciously doth rest
Upon that cloudlet in the west.
And well may he with hope and prayer
Follow the barque fast fading there.
The frail thread of her fate is one
With that of his unhappy son.

He rose, when God said to the night
Of his despair; 'Let there be light!'
And gathered all his little store
Of hoarded wealth to count it o'er.
One precious chain of shining gold—
His mother's gift, and she had told
How many generations past
Had worn the relic, she the last.

He prized it for her sake, how much!
But at this moment not even such
A thought could move. He saw with joy
How far 'twould aid to save his boy.
Another! ah, but this had laced
The bodice green his Mary wore
The hour when first a wife she blessed
The home that knoweth her no more;
And on her happy bosom lay
Those bright medallions, hanging still
Upon the links they graced that day—
Slowly the tears his sad eyes fill;
But on our isle even grief is calm;
An instant held he in his palm
The priceless chain, and then beside
His mother's, laid this of his bride.
His little flock must now be sold,
His household stuff all turned to gold;
The friendly neighbors bring their gains
To swell the sum he thus obtains.

THE RANSOM.

Into this treasury too was cast
The widow's mite, nor came she last.
The poor lorn creature we have seen
At sunset on the sandy shore
Brought all the riches that had been
Her own, and first her mother's dower;
A chain—our island maidens' pride—
And rings of antique form, beside
A silver watch her son had brought
From some strange land, she knew not what.
"Take these, good neighbor! I am reft
Of sons and daughters; none are left
To claim them when He calls me home,
And where I go these cannot come."
The goodly ransom, now all told,
A hand within that ship doth hold—
A trusty hand, pledged o'er the sea
To bear it safe to Barbary.
Alas! old man, who watchest now
With chastened joy and pious vow

Yon point that, while we speak, away
Has melted in the twilight gray,
Thy Gracious Maker hides from thee,
In love, the things which yet must be!
And we—were it not well to look
No further now in Fate's dark book,
But turn a backward glance the while
On the past fortunes of our isle!

Stand we by Wolfe upon the knoll, and turn us to the sea;
There, where the waves like breakers roll in foam so wild and free,
Stood the first church the old man knew, though parish records say
That many a goodlier one before the tide had swept away.
Even yet the shepherds deem they hear, of a still Easter morn,
The chiming of the bells full clear from the deep waves upborne,

And that at midnight when they watch by some dear pass-
    ing soul,
The listening ear may faintly catch a low and muffled toll.
'Tis said, too, when the sea is calm, that ofttimes may be
    seen
Not only the lost house of God, but buried homes of men;
That still upright beneath the flood as fair to view they stand
As when they rose upon the isle, fresh from the builder's
    hand.*

But to my tale. In that first church, upon Wolfe's infant
    head
With simple rite, the man of God Christ's covenant waters
    shed.
There with his parents, when a boy, from week to week he
    went
To pray for pardon of his sins through him whom God hath
    sent.

---

* It is reported of many of the sunken hamlets, that at times their church-bells are heard to ring beneath the water, and that in still weather, their houses can be discerned in the deep. The bells of a sunken village in North Friesland are said to chime on Easter morning.

There, men and angels witnessing, he stood in manhood's pride,
And wedded with a soul-deep vow his orphan Iceland bride.

But all these years the wasting shore was crumbling, day by day;
With purpose sure, the cruel foe aneared his trembling prey.
Each art the island knew was tried the hallowed house to save;
In vain—one night of wind and tide, it sunk beneath the wave.
Sadly at dawn they gathered there to see the ruin wrought;
The fearful sight to every heart a painful shudder brought.
The church was gone, the churchyard, too, alas! all washed away,
There scattered on the moaning beach, the broken coffins lay;
Some were still hanging to the bank from which the soil had slid,
The mouldering skeleton within seen through the shattered lid;

And bones, that loving friends had laid full tenderly to rest,
Swept far away, were rudely rocked on the rough ocean's breast.
Shocked into silence, lo! that group a moment fixed as stone!
Then sudden every bosom heaves with a half-stifled groan.
Not one but sees some sleeping friend torn from the quiet bed,
Where he had hoped to lie in peace till God should wake the dead.
The parent mourns the child anew; children for parents weep;
And spouse for spouse—their treasures safe not e'en the grave will keep.
Poor Wolfe sought vainly, as he held his trembling Mary fast,
For the pale sod that covered all save Melleff, now their last.*

* The cemeteries are often washed away, and the bodies of the dead are not unfrequently removed to a more secure resting-place when such a catastrophe threatens.

At length the pastor mildly spoke; " O little flock," he said,
" Wherefore are ye cast down, and why are ye disquieted?
The body that we sow is not the body that shall be—
So writes the apostle unto whom was shown the mystery—
With such a form as pleaseth Him our God shall clothe His saints,
He needeth not these poor remains—cease then your vain complaints!
Already round his radiant throne the Lord's redeemèd stand,
Nor fire nor flood nor death nor hell shall pluck them from His hand.
Sorrow not o'er these wave-washed bones, but rather let us pray
For everlasting freedom from the galling bonds of clay!"
They prayed; then to their common toil with lighter hearts returned,
But long and deeply for their church, pastor and people mourned.

One anxious thought filled every mind—anew how should
    they build?
No block of stone, no beam of wood, their naked soil doth
    yield;
All must be brought from other shores, nor would, for
    years, suffice
The produce of their little fold to pay the needful price.
One only source of gain, beside, their barren isle can boast;
When mighty winds, for many days, the angry waves have
    tossed,
Till the vast chambers of the deep are shaken to their base,
And then the weary sea retires to his accustomed place,
Along his track, retreating, lo! the sparkling amber spread,*
Rent and cast upward by the storm from ocean's jewelled
    bed!
Here the pure drops long ages gone were known as Freya's
    tears,
And still, passed down from sire to son, the shining treasure
    bears

* See Appendix VII.

The ancient name, though long forgot the tale from whence it sprung—
The memory of Odur's spouse has perished even from song!
Yet not less valued than of old is the fair merchandise,
And for our frugal islanders their choicest stores it buy's.
All these they gladly will resign; henceforth it is their care
To consecrate the wealth so gained to rear a house of prayer.
A few short years of sacrifice their lost church may replace;
The thought sheds joy on every heart, a smile on every face.
Whene'er the warring elements exhausted sleep once more,
Eager they seek the glittering spoil along the dripping shore.
Some search the channel's oozy bed left for a moment dry,
While others higher on the beach a safer fortune try.
And some with bolder foot press close on the receding flood,
Still watchful lest their faithless foe turn back in angry mood.
Children o'erleap the narrow creeks, light bounding to and fro,
With panting breath and burning cheeks, each new found prize to show.

Their quest they cease not till the tide, repenting his retreat,
Turns suddenly and towards their wharves drives them with flying feet.
Then with glad hearts the glowing hoard they to the pastor bear,
That he in their increasing store their modest joy may share.

So months passed on, and all the gains thus gathered from the sea
Formed still a treasury lighter far than their necessity.
The autumn, too, came on apace, and they could meet no more
To worship, where the church once stood, upon the open shore.
Yet wintry tempests, gathering strength, might scatter on the strand
The golden pebbles so desired with a more lavish hand.
Such was the talk one cold gray morn, as they drew near the sea .

Still hoarse with chafing all the night, though now no wind
    was free.
A child's swift foot that blind pursued the eye's more dis-
    tant aim,
Struck sharply on an iron ring that well might wonder
    claim.
That child was Melleff, still the first when Fortune smiled
    or frowned,
And ever for adventure strange o'er all the isle renowned.
They dug, and lo! a heavy box, strong and of curious form,
Was lifted from the solid drift packed round it by the
    storm.
They climbed the downs, and every shoal searched with a
    careful eye,
Even to the horizon's utmost verge, where wrecks were wont
    to lie.
Canvas nor mast nor hulk were there, and wasting rust told
    plain
That long upon the lonely beach that ancient chest had
    lain.

Great was the marvel, greater still when on their dazzled sight
Flashed all the riches hid within, the gold, the silver bright,
So fairly wrought that many deemed they saw the precious hoard,
That cunning dwarfs (as sagas tell) beneath the downs had stored.*

They sent the tidings far and wide, but owner never came,
Message or letter none were sent the costly prize to claim.
Who knoweth but the same wild surf that here the chest had rolled,
Choked into silence every voice that might its tale have told?
At length the glittering toys were sold. O! what a joy to find
The little church might now be built for which they so had pined.
For greater safety from the sea, another site they chose
Behind the downs, and rapidly the humble walls arose.

* A similar incident actually occurred on one of these islands.

Years passed; full many a wharf had bowed before the
    tyrant flood,
And still unharmed by wind or wave that sanctuary stood.
Yet, ah! such changes time had wrought among the shifting
    downs,
That in a foe till now unfeared a sure destruction frowns.
In vain with tireless zeal they strive to avert the stern decree,
Onward the mighty sandwave rolls resistless as the sea.
Slowly it creepeth up the walls, it gathers round the door,
Sifts through the casements' guarded seams, and thickly
    strews the floor.
Long did they clear, from week to week, the swelling heaps
    away,
Meeting within those hallowed courts each blessed sabbath
    day.
But ever higher rose the sand, defying human strength;
It reached the seats, the pastor's desk, and choked the door
    at length.

* For an account of a church buried in this way by the sand, see Appendix VIII.

To a new entrance, thus enforced, a window they transform;
Still is the shelter of the roof more welcome than the storm.
There at the patient pastor's feet gathered the little band
Of tried and faithful worshippers, no cushion but the sand.
There lifted they their hearts to Him who once in meekness made
Himself the Son of man, and had not where to lay his head.

O child of wealth! the portals high of a cathedral pile
Stand wide for thee, and thou dost sweep through the long pillared aisle,
With dainty foot, and jewelled hand, in raiment rich and rare,
To rest on swelling velvet soft, through a brief hour of prayer.
Yet to have faith like one of these, if thou but knew its worth,
Thou'dst gladly give thy place for his upon the dusty earth.

And thou to whom the lines have fallen God's word to minister

In pleasant places to the rich, of thine own soul have care!
See that thou miss not the bright crown of glory only worn
By those who first the bitter cross of sacrifice have borne.
Oppressed with solitude and want, behold thy brother stand,
Feeding with zeal the humble flock committed to his hand!
Possessed, it may be, of a mind as richly stored as thine,
Gifted with kindling eloquence, where thought and grace
    combine,
That well might challenge the applause of audience more fit,
And draw admiring crowds to praise his wisdom and his
    wit:
Yet, prompt to do his Master's will, he asks of man no meed—
Of such a stimulus to toil hast thou as little need?
Boldly against a nation's sin thou dost not spare to cry;
'Tis well! God help thee! lift thy voice in trumpet tones
    on high,
Until our land repent her crimes!—and yet who will not
    own
'Tis easier far such war to wage where thousands shout,
    "well done!"

Than thus, an exile from the world, in such a waste obscure,
Death threatening in each rising gale, with patience to endure
Privation, labor, loneliness, no witness to applaud,
Save his own conscience and the eye, all-seeing, of his God.

The autumn wind, that mournfully had sighed all day, sobbed still
More loudly and grew passionate as night's gray shadows fell.
Low mist-like clouds rolled rapidly over the evening sky,
And a yet darker mask was seen through their thin drapery,
So thick that neither moon nor stars could pierce it with a ray,
Nor through its heavy folds had shot one beam of parting day.
Like a tired beast of prey, for hours the sluggish sea had slept,
And scarce would heed the driving winds that o'er its bosom swept.

But when the gathering darkness came, its deep and sullen roar,
More dreadful than the shrieking gale, shook all the trembling shore.
Long, long, and fearful was the night, but when, with languid smile
And tardy wing, the morning rose upon the drenched isle,
The winds were hushed; not so the dash of the far sounding sea,
Toward which the anxious shepherds looked with kindly sympathy.
There, beating on a fatal shoal, a noble vessel lay,
And high above her stately decks was tossed the snow-white spray.
A moment more, a sturdy boat, strong arms at every oar,
Is flying toward the stranded ship where loud the breakers roar.
Now, God be thanked! the gallant craft is not a hopeless wreck;
The weary crew are standing safe upon the sloping deck.

With shouts they hail the barque that braves for them so
    wild a sea,
Bold Wolfe, the pilot, pledged himself to set the vessel free
At evening tide—so well he knew what change of wind was
    near—
And bade the troubled mariners dismiss each anxious fear.
At sunset rose the swelling tide, the breeze set from the
    land,
Another hour, and the good ship was floated from the sand,
And, wisely steered by him who knew the perils of that
    shore,
Threaded the crooked channel safe, and stood to sea once
    more.

Weeks passed—broad broken bands of ice behind the island
    stretch,
So that however great the need, none might the mainland
    reach.
Though want, disease and death draw nigh, succor they may
    have none,

Other than this poor sod affords, except from God alone.*

And yet their childlike faith in Him forbids each anxious fear,

For though they know their brethren far, they feel their Father near.

With patient, but with longing hearts, they wait the coming spring;

Even to this barren wilderness new pleasures doth she bring.

True, here she comes not garlanded with the bright flowers she loves,

And drawn by throngs of singing birds, like Venus by her doves;

But smoother seas and brighter skies her gentle heralds are,

And yet more welcome still the news she brings from friends afar.

---

* In the autumn the single wharfs are often separated from each other by the tide, and in the winter, the ice sometimes cuts them off from the mainland for weeks together. The isolation of the Halligs is most deeply felt in case of sickness. They are then obliged to send across the oozy flats, a distance of twenty or thirty miles, for medical advice and attendance, but even this is possible only in favorable weather.—Weigelt, die Nordfriesischen Inseln, 20.

Parents, whose hardy sons have sought their fortune on the deep,
Maidens, whose lovers toil abroad while they must wait and weep,
The pastor linked to the great world by every tender tie
That binds the memory to the past—all these for tidings sigh.
They come—alas 'tis ever so! some weep while others smile;
Yet to the hand of Wolfe was brought a joy for all the isle.
The wealthy owner of the ship late stranded on this coast,
And which but for his timely aid had surely there been lost.
Such generous recompense has sent for succor promptly given,
As well may serve to rear a house to the great God of Heaven.
This his first thought. With clamorous tongue he pleads no special right,
But in one purpose, with one voice, like brothers all unite.
" The Lord hath touched the stranger's heart. How wondrous are his ways!
Another temple to His name with joyful hands we'll raise."

'Twas done. Wild, desolating floods have o'er the island rolled
Full oft since then, not sparing even the shepherd and his fold.
That church still stands, and, to the eyes of those who worship there,
Its simple walls and humble spire are objects not less fair
Than Zion's towers and bulwarks seemed to Israel's shepherd king,
When by her glorious beauty moved such strains of praise to sing.

CANTO VI.

THE CARAVAN.

LAND of the pyramid! land of the palm!
Fanning us now with thy breezes of balm,
Lovely thou art, and yet stranger than fair!
Glamour is with thee, and whoso shall dare
Look on thy beauty will know never more
Rest, till the throb of his last pulse is o'er! *
Long since thy vassals, why shudder we then,
Feeling thy breath on our foreheads again?
Angels of God! that in nightly patrol
Wheel round our planet from pole unto pole,
Hovering now o'er yon desolate isle,
Now where the date-groves of Barbary smile,

* Niemand wandelt unter Palmen ungestraft.

There, whispering soft to the meek as they sleep,
Here, frowning darkly on robbers that creep
Forth in the midnight, dividing their prey—
Do ye not sorrow to turn you away
Thus, from the dwelling of peace, to the shore
Echoing with tumult and strife evermore—
Hither, where hearts through their pride have grown
    cold,
Shrivelled and seared by the lust after gold?
Oh, not the brightness, that Israel's way
Guided in glory by night and by day,
Fired him with courage unflinching to bear
Pains that here lightly for Mammon they dare!
Man's eager hand from that glittering fleece
Fear cannot hold, nor sweet pity release!
Yet will we follow where Melleff, the slave,
Pineth for home, and imploreth a grave.

Behold Tunisia's towers once more,
See through her Gate of Plenty pour

Camels and men, a ceaseless tide,
First a dense line, then—spreading wide
Like a full stream that doth o'erflow
Its banks, and fill the vale below—
They roll adown the rocky steep,
And the wide olive-plains o'ersweep.

To-day the merchant caravan *
Its yearly march to far Soudan
Begins. Beneath a flaming sky
Its long and perilous way doth lie
O'er Sahara's boundless, pathless plains,
Where wild, unchanging horror reigns.
The adventurer, who shall safely reach
Nigritia's border, thence may fetch—
The price of trifles worthless nigh
To all but the untutored eye,

---

* The reader will find a full account of the organization and march of the great caravans engaged in the Soudan trade, in Le Grand Désert ou Itinéraire d'une Caravane du Sahara au pays des Nègres, par Eugene Daumas, et Ausone de Chancel. Paris, 1848.

Or a few handfuls of the weed
Scarce sanctioned by the Moslem creed—*
Treasures which kings would gladly own.
'Neath sacks of gold his camels groan,—
Those shining sands the Jinn have rolled
From mountain caverns dark and cold,
Down crystal streams to plains below,
There in the tropic fires to glow;
Her plumes are from the ostrich rent,
Nor spared the lordly elephant.
Even man—his brother man—the pains
Of death must feel, to swell his gains.
Tribe against tribe doth lift the spear,
None deems a trinket bought too dear,
If but some wretched captive may
The price with life-long service pay.

---

* It was long a question among the doctors of the Mohammedan law whether tobacco was not virtually forbidden to the faithful, as an intoxicating drug. The use of tobacco was made a highly penal offence by some of the Turkish sultans.

Yet leave such thoughts, and mark how bright
The landscape glows in morning light!
Oh, 'tis a wondrous show and fair,
The living picture painted there!
All the vast crowd clad in a guise
Strange to the Frank's unwonted eyes;
The scarlet fez, the white bernous,
The gay keffieh floating loose,
With its long fringes light and free
By every breeze tossed gracefully;
The sash that in its brilliant folds
The Arab's choicest treasures holds,
His yataghan, with massive hilt,
His heavy pistols richly gilt;
The spahi to rough battle bred,
With tufted lance and mantle red;
Wild horsemen flying like the wind,
Their wide robes streaming far behind;
Steeds, whose rich trappings well may vie
With their gay riders' bravery,

And in whose kindling eye there glares
The same wild light that burns in theirs;
And scarce less prized, with foot as light,
The young mehari creamy white,
Her saddle with full tassels hung,
Her neck with polished cowries strung;
There the grave camel pensive stands,
As dreaming of the endless sands,
That he, with laden step, must tread,
The vulture hovering o'er his head.

But lo, the pacha and his train
Wind down the pathway to the plain.
Hareem, guard, servants, form his suite,
All ordered with a splendor meet
For Eastern despot, when he goes
In search of pleasure, not of foes.
When the date-harvest draweth nigh,
It is the pacha's wont to fly
From cares of state, awhile to rest

In Nefta's * gardens, rich and blest

As groves of the Hesperides,

Whose golden apples Gods could please.

There soars the palm of loftiest shoot,

Of broadest leaf, and choicest fruit;

Nor this alone, but every tree,

Shrub, vine, most prized by luxury.

Now, when the caravan affords

Sure guard against the robber-hordes,

Thither the pleasure-loving Bey

With friends and followers takes his way,

To linger there till Spring's bright train

Makes Tunis paradise again.

A jet-black courser doth he ride,

That bears his lord with conscious pride;

A nobler steed, as all may see,

---

* Nefta, the Negeta of the Romans, a town of 3000 inhabitants, lies south-west of Tunis, and is remarkable for the abundance and excellent quality of its waters, its olives, its dates, its pomegrantes, its melons, and, in short, all the vegetable productions of the climate. The Bey of Tunis has a palace at Nefta, and formerly made it his winter residence.

Was never bred in Araby.
And close at hand, the aatoosh shows
Its silken curtains, that enclose
The bright Messouda, the young wife
Of Aali, precious as his life.
Another—this his daughter bears,
The lovely Fatmeh, now of years
More womanly, and with a light
Of beauty lent to mortal sight
But rarely. To the childlike grace,
That ever marks the Eastern maid,
Is added, in that matchless face,
Of earnestness a tender shade.
Whence came that beam of heavenly thought
To one by book or sage untaught,
And in a false religion bred?
Be not so narrow in thy creed!
The God, who Job and Abram loved,
Although their people knew Him not,
Who Moab's gentle daughter moved,

Though Moab had His name forgot,
Hath still His own in every land
Taught by His voice led by His hand!

Old Gerda at the maiden's side
Beholds her with a mother's pride;
Their talk is of the late demand
Made by Algeria's tyrant lord,
Stern Ibrahim, for Fatmeh's hand,
To which the Bey will not accord;
And much the grateful daughter fears
Her father's pity for her tears
May kindle war's devouring flame—
'Then hers the sin and hers the shame!'

Behind the women came a troop
Of slaves—a strangely mingled group,
Together brought o'er land and sea,
Of every faith and every kin,
From Ethiop's darkest ebony
To Europe's fairest, rosiest skin.

Above the rest, young Melleff's form
Towered high, as doth the forest tree
Over the brushwood, though the storm
May bow its head full heavily.
His foot is lingering, and his eye
Turned backward to the Northern sky;
For each reluctant step removes
Him further from the home he loves.
Alas! he may no more delay;
The caravan is on its way!
Allah hoo akbar! how the cry
Swells upward, as 'twould rend the sky!
Now, now, must friends their farewells speak,
Not wives—they make the heart too weak.
Sadly the parting words are said,
Sires bless their sons, with hands outspread,
Mothers and sisters weeping loud,
With their full pitchers, through the crowd
Are hurrying, water fresh to throw
Upon the camels ere they go;

Then gather, with a trembling hand
And tearful eye, the trodden sand,
Where the departing foot was set,
To wear it for an amulet;
Praying it may be Allah's will
Their friends should meet no omen ill,
No slave deformed, nor men at strife,
Nor raven boding loss of life;
Rather a warrior richly clad,
Or a young matron gay and glad,
Who her soft girdle will unbind,
And give it fluttering to the wind,
To insure for them a safe return,
And for herself a gift to earn.
Meanwhile, the human flood sweeps on
Through olive-groves, rough steeps adown,
Through viny vales, o'er sandy wastes,
Alternate, till at length it rests
Beneath the walls of old Zowan;
There sleeps the weary caravan.

O Melleff! had the pictured scroll
Of Time's strange tale ere met thine eye,
The anguish of thy fainting soul
Thou wouldst forget, where thou dost lie,
Gazing on Zowan's towering crest
Now in its sunset glory dressed.

Hark! from yon frowning heights dost thou not hear
Voices unearthly through the gathering gloom,
So low and mournful, that the listening ear
Knows them but echoes from the hollow tomb?

Alas, we cannot catch the words they speak!
From lips of such ethereal essence light,
Our heavy, cloddish senses are too weak
To guess the mystic meaning half aright.

Oh, for the gift divine, late dreamers claim,
With souls departed converse free to hold!
Then would we bid the dead of olden fame
Come nearer, and the mighty past unfold.

Ye stolèd priests, who erst majestic trod
Those peaks sublime, with hymn and offering due
To greet Phœnicia's bright and burning god,
When o'er them his first ray and last he threw;

Who lingered still, when his glad beams were gone,
To welcome great Astarte, queen of Heaven,
That, crescent-crowned, shot from her sapphire throne
A light which paled the fairest star of even;

What Orient land was first your father's nurse?
How had they thus Jehovah's name forgot,
Who to the sun gives his appointed course,
And the moon seasons that she passes not?

Tell us of Dido, young and lovely queen,
Wherefore an exile from the Tyrian shore?
Or, was she but a phantom only seen
In the fond poet's visionary lore?

Sicilia's tyrant, fierce Agathocles!
How looked great Carthage, when from yonder mount
Thou didst survey, with anxious, longing eyes,
This tempting vale, and war's stern chances count? *

What arts have flourished, ere the Roman sword,
With jealous hate accursed, laid all so low?
And was indeed this ancient empire's word
As worthless as the faith of nations now?

Alas, there comes no answer all the night!
In vain we summon him called African,
And him of Utica, though well they might
Still linger where their deathless fame began.

Even Hippo's bishop will not hear our prayer!
He, open once as truth—though we entreat

---

* It was from the peak of Zowan that, according to Diodorus Siculus, Agathocles viewed both Carthage and Hadrumetum in that bold campaign, when in the midst of the siege of Syracuse by the Carthaginians, he secretly left the city, and landed with a considerable force, near the enemy's capital in Africa, and after many brilliant victories, nearly succeeded in capturing it.

With passion unto tears—deigns not declare
What now he would retract, and what repeat.

Let us then trace those streams of crystal sheen
To their high sources in the mountain's breast.
Will they not tell us what strange things have been,
Since first their sparkling floods these valleys blest?

No! Ammon's temple * even is silent now,
With none to tell who bade its mighty heart
Send forth the tide, whose full and lengthening flow
To thirsty Carthage did its wealth impart.

Alas! we find no teacher 'neath the skies,
Save giant skeletons of empires dead!
May yet some great historic Cuvier rise,
New light, from these, on ages past to shed!

* The temple of Jupiter Ammon, the walls of which are still standing, is the most important of the ruins of Zowan. The temple was a sort of *chateau d'eau*, containing an immense basin for receiving the waters of the fountains, and delivering them into the aqueduct, which, by a circuitous route of fifty miles, conveyed them to Carthage.

But the poor captive had no dreams
Like these. Far other were the themes
That fed his fancy, as he lay
Dreading yet longing for the day.
A vision of the night revealed
Ere sleep had once his eye-lids sealed—
As then undoubtingly he deemed—
And which so true, so life-like seemed,
Now with confusion clouds his brain—
He thinks it o'er and o'er again.
Robed, voiced like woman, it drew near
His side and bade him—"Be of cheer!
Nor longer mourn thy mother's fears,
For God hath dried her many tears!
The sunset of thy father's day
Thou yet may'st brighten—hope and pray!
Even here doth love still watch o'er thee,
With purpose strong to set thee free!"

He tried to speak—the figure fast
Melted away, and all was passed!

Day comes—not with a lingering foot,
As in the chill and misty North,
But suddenly its red beams shoot
Athwart the sky, and o'er the earth.
Then all is bustle in the camp,
Of man and beast a hurried tramp.
The camels groan with rage and pain
To feel the hated load again.
The driver's curse rings loud and clear;
O'er all, the voice of the Khrebir,
Bidding the lagging line move on,
Ere the fresh morning hour be gone.
Now, through the fertile vale they wind,
But soon must leave its wealth behind.
To-day their toilsome journey leads
O'er arid sands, through rocky beds
Of torrents bare, so rough and steep,

The camel scarce his foot may keep.
But in the desert, at this hour,
The wanderer feels unwonted power.
He counteth not the weary leagues,
Recks not of dangers or fatigues.
How doth the heart of Ishmael's child
Bound, to behold his native wild
In the fair morning light spread out!
He fills the air with song and shout!

Oh, would'st thou taste the highest bliss
That freedom on the soul bestows,
Go forth into the wilderness,
When the first day-born zephyr blows!
There shalt thou feel thy Psyche-wings
Lift thee above all earthly things!
But ah, they shall not bear thee long,
For Phœbus, wroth at human pride,
Will smite thee, with a beam as strong
As that by which young Icarus died,

And thou shalt fall to earth again,
A mortal wrung with want and pain!

Even Melleff felt his heart more light
Than 'neath the curtain of the night;
There seemed a tender presence near,
That with sweet promise filled his ear—
Promise of liberty and home!
Thought of his mother scarce was gloom—
Not greatly generous hearts complain
For those for whom to die is gain.—
That midnight whisper, breathing low
Of cheer and love—oh, might he know
If it were hers! he will obey,
Howe'er it be, and hope and pray!
With clearer brow and footstep strong
He follows now that servile throng.

Heavily doth the mid-day pass,
When earth and heaven alike are brass.

The Arab's song is hushed; no sound
Breaketh the awful stillness round,
Save the slow camel's drowsy tread
Across the plain so dry and dead,
And the sand's rustle, falling back
As the foot leaves the indented track.
There is no shade in earth or sky,
On which to rest the aching eye.
On every side a fiery glare,
A quivering glimmer in the air,
As if even air would waste away
In that fierce, endless noontide ray!
The glowing sands are heavenward whirled
In lofty columns tinged with flame,
As if from out the kindling world
The smoke of its last burning came!
Poor Melleff, late of strength so high,
Now child-weak, faints as death were nigh.
But see, across his languid face
A sudden flush of rapture pass!

He lifts his sinking head, and cries:
" Lo, yonder the fair water lies!"
Not gladder those old Greeks than he,
When first they saw 'the sea! the sea!'
Alas, O Melleff, thou art mocked!
Those towers, that lake, those boats wave-rocked,
Those islands plumed with forests tall—
They are but empty phantoms all!
Would we with words that fancy cure?
As well bid the young heart be sure
Life will not her fair promise keep,
But leave all eyes at last to weep!
Oh, 'tis not thus that we may learn
Our souls from vanity to turn;
Each for himself must test the show,
And truth by stern experience know.
Oft must the desert-wanderer prove
The stately castle, verdant grove,
The clear, bright lake, the boundless sea,
To be a cruel mockery,

Before those cheating shadows will
Cease with vain hopes his soul to fill!

Lo, fading is that vision fair!
There is a light stir in the air,
A faint, hot sigh, and all again
Is still—as vainly nature then
Strove to dissolve the fatal spell,
And back to endless silence fell.
Another—a more stifling blast,
Now gust on gust is following fast!
'Tis the thick breath of the simoom,
In cloudy volumes rolling by,
Filling the air with lurid gloom
That shrouds alike the earth and sky.
The camels from the smothering gale
Turn gasping, while the Arabs veil
With thickest folds the averted face,
And man and beast stand motionless.
Fierce was the sand-storm—but soon past;

Again the slow lines onward stretch

In moody silence, till at last

The longed-for resting-place they reach;

While, sun-touched still, the eye may scan

The far-off towers of Kairouan.*

Beneath a thin acacia's shade,

The captive laid his burning head,

And prayed for death. His weary feet

Were blistered by the scorching heat

Of flint and sand, through which, unshod,

With bleeding step he long had trod.

Speechless, the parched and stiffened tongue

To the mouth dry and fevered clung;

The swollen, cracked lips were purple grown,

The eyes, that once as purely shone

As sapphire in a crystal sea,

Had lost their dewy brilliancy;

---

* Kairouan, situated in a sterile sandy plain, almost entirely without vegetation, was the African capital of the Moslem conquerors in the eighth and ninth centuries.

The glazed and heavy orbs, grown dim,
Seemed in a pool of blood to swim;
A fiery current coursed each vein,
With quick, hot throbbings beat his brain,
Bewildered thought from side to side
Flew hurriedly, but nought descried
Save threatening phantoms of distress,
Then sank to dark unconsciousness.
Around the sleeper all is life,
Command, and curse, and quarrel rife.
The Bey's green tents are pitched in haste,
With care mats, skins and cushions placed.
But for the rest, a single man
Alone of all the caravan
May claim such comforts—the Khrebir,
The leader whom they all revere—
For well they know the proverb wise,
That thus the Arab doth advise:
'If thou must needs a journey make,
Then to thyself companions take.

Alone, a demon doth pursue;

With pilgrims twain are tempters two;

And when the number swells to three,

Let one the chosen chieftain be.' *

To him they give obedience meet,

Spread the soft carpet for a seat,

And shelter him from cold and heat.

Some from their loads the camels free,

And bind with cords the bended knee,

That none from the encampment stray,

And to marauders fall a prey.

The slaves are scattered o'er the plain

In eager search—nor quite in vain,—

For desert-shrubs that serve to light

The needful watchfires of the night,

And with whose brisk and crackling blaze,

Though short-lived, they have learned to raise

---

* The Prophet has said: "Begin your journeys on Friday, and always with company. Alone, a demon follows you; if ye are two, two demons do tempt you; and when ye are three, choose to you a chief."

The steaming odors, that so deep
In Mocha's priceless berry sleep.
Its fragrance now is on the air,
And straight the tiny cup they bear
To their tired lords, who glad lay by
Their pipes for this blest luxury.
The servants then their thirst assuage
With the same precious beverage.
This done, the savory meats they dress,
By Arabs of the wilderness
So prized. Meanwhile, from her employ
A negro girl young Fatmeh calls,
And bids her nurse the Christian boy.
Upon her knee Ayesha falls
Beside that form insensible,
And marks the troubled breathing well.
Then lifting from the torrid sand
The languid head, with gentle hand,
Gives to his lips the welcome draught,
Which but half consciously is quaffed.

When from the sky the red sun passed,
And night with sudden chill came fast,
O'er him the warm caftan she spread,
A folded mat sustained his head,
And blessed sleep soon chased away
The image of that fearful day.

Now bright the ruddy camp-fires burn!
Around, the watchers, each in turn,
Tell their wild tales of love or war,
Or hidden treasures,* such as are
Only to Christian magi known,
And at whose potent call alone
The gorgeous jewels will gush forth,
In shining streams, from the dark earth;
Then on the sparkling flood shall roll,
Nor mountain bar nor sea control,
Till it hath reached the Christian shore,

---

* Traditions of immense treasure hidden in the depths of the earth, or inclosed in the solid rock, and which can be discovered only by Christian sages, are very current in Africa.

On Frankistan its wealth to pour—
Whose voice upon the night doth break?
"Ho, watchman! sleep ye now or wake?"
They know their faithful leader's cry,
And with assuring shouts reply,
Retrim the wasting fires, and then
Take up the half-told tale again.
But hark! from out the circling gloom,
A note that shakes like trump of doom!
Watchers and sleepers at the sound
Start to their feet with headlong bound;
The ready muskets blazing ring
On every side; the watch-fires fling
Their mounting wings of crimson light
Far out upon the sullen night;
The camel with deep shuddering moans
The presence of his monarch owns,
While human shouts ascending high
Declare that nobler man is nigh,
And warn the royal beast to fly.

He hears—he that for peer alone

The son of woman deigns to own—*

Nor for such foe will longer stay,

But back to darkness stalks away.

---

* When the lion roars, the Arabs pretend to distinguish the words "ahna ou ben el mera. I and the son of the woman." Ahna (I) he utters but once, but he repeats "the son of the woman," whence it is inferred that he recognizes man as his superior.

CANTO VII.

THE LETTER.

Let us fly from the burning desert forth,
For an hour to the cool and showery North!
From the jackal's cry, from the lion's roar,
To the billows that break on a troubled shore—
Hear the scream of the sea-mew wild, instead
Of the vulture's flap o'er the carcass dead—
Leave the sandy couch, where the captive sleeps,
For the knoll where his watch the father keeps!

There still the patient father stands
Where first we marked him, on the down,
And of each passing sail demands
If it bear tidings of his son.

THE LETTER.

Again the fair midsummer-tide
Shines, as when Melleff left his side,
So bold, so full of hope to earn
Such mead for toils he longed to bear,
That he full shortly might return
To free his father's age from care!
Where is he now? how deep this thought
In every feature is inwrought!
But on that withered cheek a beam
Of fresher hue methinks doth glow.
Oh, is it not the trembling gleam
Reflected from hope's radiant bow?
Aye, and his eye is dim and bright
By turns from that same changeful light.
Hath some late news of his lost boy
Shed on his heart this doubtful joy?

But see! he leaves the twilight shore,
Across the winding creek is gone
Toward a kind neighbor's friendly door,
6*

That never bar or bolt hath known.
A moment let us enter there,
Before the guest's slow foot draws nigh.
It is the hour of evening prayer,
And its deep tones fill solemnly
The hushed space of the dusky room,
Half-curtained by the twilight gloom;
But still around each kneeler's head
A shimmer of the evening red
Doth linger. By its fading light
Their number we may tell aright.
The father first, whose silver hair
Gleams like a saintly glory there,
And near him, touched by the same ray,
A child's unquiet tresses play.
Next, side by side, two sisters meek
A blessing on the absent seek,
Each in a mourning vesture clad—
Well may they wear those garments sad!
A husband's coming one doth wait;

THE LETTER.

The other for a lover sighs
Whose parting sail to-day was set,
Just lost to her pursuing eyes.
Are there no more? A low amen
Comes from a shadowy corner, when
The father's simple prayer is done—
It is the mother's feeble tone!
Within that arm-chair—curious wrought
By hands that have their craft forgot
For centuries—sits the aged dame,
And thus hath sat for years the same.
Ere icy-fingered Time could dare
To frost one thread of her dark hair,
Or draw one line across the brow
So deeply scored with furrows now,
The arrows of disease pierced sore
That shrinking frame, and evermore
His patient thrall she bideth still,
Waiting with cheerful courage, till

He who set Abraham's daughter free,
Loose her from her infirmity.

Soon as the worshippers arise,
The glad child to the window flies,
And, leaning through the open sash,
Watches the billows' foamy dash,
But, most of all, the evening sky,
That seldom glows so ruddily
Around the chill and misty isle,
Though warmed by summer's softest smile.
A growing wonder shades the joy
Spread o'er the features of the boy.
"O, grandpapa! now tell me, pray,
Who takes the golden sun away,
And keeps it from us all the night?
And what makes yonder sky so bright?"
As moved by some lost memory,
The old man smiled, then on his knee

The little questioner he set,
And to his daughter playful turned,
Whose cheeks with recent tears were wet,—
" Come, Ola! hear a tale I learned
Long since; 'tis one will suit thee well,
Sit thou beside me while I tell!"

MIDSUMMER TWILIGHT.

Thou seest in the West, where the waves wash the sky,
The torch of the day-star at eve slow expiring;
Again dost behold, with thine opening eye,
His flambeau rekindled, the Orient firing.

Hath any e'er shown thee, who quencheth its light?
E'er told thee of Quelling, the maiden immortal?
Of Delling, the youth, with his locks amber-bright,
Who bears it, relighted, through Morn's flashing portal?

Then hear how the bards of the North tell the tale:
When Allfather's work of creation was ended,
That daylight and darkness in turn should not fail,
He called two fair spirits that round him attended.

To rosy young Quelling, his loveliest child,
A virgin whose birthright was beauty eternal,
He spoke thus, in accents paternally mild:
"My daughter, behold, this thy duty diurnal—

"To extinguish the torch of the westering Sun,
When earthward he leaneth, with face flushed and weary;
And keep it with care till the dew-beaded dawn
Shall scatter dun Night, with her train pale and dreary."

To Delling, the first of the heavenly choir:
"Thine be it, when Sol starteth up from his sleeping,
To bid the torch flame with ethereal fire,
And give it again to his watchfullest keeping."

The fair sky-born children since, ever in turn,
Have failed not to do as Allfather hath bidden;
At dawn, heaven and earth in the new glory burn —
At evening, the red blaze is carefully hidden.

When Nature, grown drowsy and chill, seeketh rest,
The torch for long hours in deep darkness reposes;
For early its beam goeth out in the West,
And late in the East, Morn's cold eyelid uncloses.

When Spring's breath requickens each life-gifted thing,
And Summer hath need of the days long and sunny,
Her flowers and her fruits to perfection to bring,
Ripe cherries for robins, for bees the sweet honey—

Then early and late stands the Sun in the skies,
Still pouring his warm rays on meadow and river;—
To paint rose and lily with loveliest dyes,
And gild the bright cornfield, he wearieth never.

Brief then are the moments of silence and shade,
Still flickers the torch just inverted by Quelling,
When clear the birds' matin-song swells from the glade,
The fire glows again, held aloft by blithe Delling.

It chanced at this sweetest of seasons, more praised,
More sung by the poets than ever another,
The watchers, star-crowned, once too earnestly gazed,
Too long, in the clear, deep, brown eyes of each other.

When Delling reached forth for the languishing flame,
He pressed the white hand that the maiden extended,
Then forward he stooped, and his ruddy lips came
Nigh-hers and more nigh, till in kisses they blended.

On Quelling's soft cheek burneth crimson a blush,
Till, skyward reflected, it reaches the zenith;
There mirrored, the fire of the youth meets the flush,
As over her beauty still fondly he leaneth.

But Odin, whose eye doth not slumber for aye,
In midnight's short silence looked down on their meeting;
He called them before him, when shone the full day,
And spake to them thus, with right fatherly greeting:

"My children, with zeal my behest ye fulfil,
And service so faithful its recompense claimeth,
Nor fear that with me it doth argue aught ill,
That Love's sacred spark your young bosom inflameth.

" Henceforth will I grant you, a true wedded pair,
Forever to dwell in a union unending,
Together all duty, all pleasure to share,
Still closer and closer your souls ever blending."

The lovers were silent—then lowly they knelt—
" Allfather forgive—hear the prayer that we offer!
Such bliss in the kiss of betrothal we felt,
We would not exchange it for all thou dost proffer.

"Oh, grant us forever affianced to live,
And yearly, when Earth in her summer robe dresses,
For largess more ample, this simple boon give,
Our hands let us join, let our lips meet in kisses!"

Then Allfather smiled on the suppliant pair,
And blessed the sweet bond of their hearts' happy choosing—
Could any who heard them breathe forth that meek prayer,
A joy such as theirs think it blame to fear losing?

Ever since, when their season of tryst cometh round,
Kind Nature pours forth her best treasures to grace it,
Her brightest of beauty, her sweetest of sound,
And ne'er suffers frost or chill mist to deface it.

Know, then, when thou seest still at midsummer's tide
A flush in the West, when the red dawn is breaking,
'Tis the glow of the youth, 'tis the blush of his bride,
New troth-vows the lovers immortal are making!*

---

* The Legend of the Midsummer Twilight is given in Kohl II., 278. It is of Esthonian origin, and the names of the youth and maiden are Koit

Wearily up the cottage mound
Old Wolfe, with feeble footsteps, wound,
And now within the door doth stand,
And now receives the welcoming hand.
" Neighbor, my errand thou canst guess!
Have patience with my childishness,
And, prithee, let me hear once more
What thou hast read me o'er and o'er
Of my poor boy. I cannot choose
But marvel that he sends no news
From his own hand. The boy could write
Fair as the pastor; and when night
Her curtains dark doth downward roll,
Strange doubts arise within my soul,

and Aemmarik. These names are, like Equotuticum—quod versu dicere non est—not well suited to English verse, and therefore the author has substituted for them Delling (Icelandic Dellingr, formed from dagr, *day*, the appellation of the Scandinavian god of day, and Quelling, a corresponding derivative from qveld (kveld, qvölld), *evening*. Those unacquainted with the Northern languages may suppose it a violation of costume to employ *Sol* as the name of the sun in a story with a Scandinavian machinery; but the sun is called Sol in Icelandic as well as in Latin.

Misgivings, fears that will not end—"
"Thy letter, daughter!" said the friend.
The youthful matron pushed aside her wheel,
And brought, with wifely pride,
The sheet that, in its careful folds,
Treasures of love and promise holds.
Thus writes the husband: "If God please,
We soon shall leave the Midland seas
For home. Young Melleff, sought in vain
So long, is found, is free again,
And in our ship for Hamburg sails.
Heaven speed her on with favoring gales!"

CANTO VIII.

THE CHASE.

'Neath Nefta's palms they slowly walked—
The foster-mother and her child—
And earnestly together talked,
While ruddy morning round them smiled.
" The Christian Melleff," said the maid,
" We miss from haunts where late he strayed.
The roses on the outer wall,
That were his charge to train and dress,
Upon the earth neglected fall—
The garden grows a wilderness.
Hath sickness smitten?—or thy hands—
O Gerda! have they loosed his bands?"

"Nay! nay! these hands in youth were found
Too weak to burst the cords that bound.
Now, trembling fast with age and pain,
How should they break another's chain?
I too have questioned, and they say
He stands of late before the Bey.
For Fatmeh! know, I more than share
For Melleff all thy watchful care.
Child of my poor lost child, to me
Dearer than all on earth save thee!—
Thou hast no words for wonder! stay—
My tale thou'lt hear another day.
Enough, enough, that now I show
One chapter of my early woe.
They tore me from my babe, my joy—
Her, since the mother of this boy—
From him I learned that mother's name,
Her orphan state, and whence she came.
Then through my soul there shot a light,
As if the noon should flash on night.

I thought—age too hath dreams so wild—
I might again behold my child,
With Melleff go—his freedom won—
And to her arms restore her son!
Breathless I sought the crowded quay
Where many a merchant flag waved free,
One from the North—the master ' well
Knew Wolfe and would not fail to tell
Of his boy's bondage;' "Ah," he cried,
"Now is it well the mother died
Ere this could reach her!"—"Is she dead?"
Gaspingly, shudderingly I said.
He answered, and I turned, once more
All crushed and hopeless, from the shore.—
Peace has returned. Now am I blest
To know my Mary is at rest.
I follow soon—but I would see,
Ere I depart, her Melleff free!
No ransom comes—and thou, once more,
O Fatmeh, shalt the Bey implore.

Where childhood's timid prayers could fail,
Thy woman's tears may still prevail "—
Young Fatmeh's face grew deadly pale.

"Up ye now! saddle the steeds that are fleetest!
Steeds for the chase of the camel-bird meetest!
See that my tents fleck the desert's red border
Ere the gray nightfall!"—so ran the Bey's order.

Ere the gray nightfall, his green tents were planted
Far to the south, where the setting sun slanted
Arrows of fire o'er a golden-waved ocean
Solid as jasper, no sound and no motion.

Far to the south, where the clouds yester-even
Marshalled their ranks by the light of the levin;
Thither the rain-loving ostrich hath sped her,
Swift as the flash of the bright bolt that led her.*

---

* The ostrich is generally found where showers of rain have lately fallen. According to the Arabs, when the ostrich sees the lightning and a gathering storm, she runs in the direction where it appears, however distant it may be. A ten days' journey (of a caravan) is but a trifle for her. They say of a man who is skilful in providing for his flocks in the desert, "He is like the ostrich; where he sees the lightning flash, there he is."

Fleet is the game they will hunt on the morrow;
Rider and horse, let them hasten to borrow
Strength from repose, ere the white robe of morning,
Seen from afar, of the chase giveth warning.

Wake! for her silvery mantle is gleaming,
O'er it her tresses of amber are streaming,
Upward on iris-hued pinions she springeth,
Pearls o'er oasis and palm-grove she flingeth!

Cast off the haïk! Be your girdle the tightest,
Saddle and bridle and stirrup the lightest,
Look to the weight of the weapon ye carry,
Lose not a moment! Lo, yonder the quarry!

Swift as a shaft from the bow of Apollo,
Forth darts the ostrich, the snorting steeds follow;
Sail-like, her white, curling pinions she spreadeth—
Is it the earth, or the air that she treadeth?

Fast on her foremost pursuer she gaineth,
Vainly each nerve and each muscle he straineth,
Vainly, with nostrils dilated, he drinketh
Draughts of the wind *—lo, he reeleth, he sinketh!

Mark how the wile of the sportsman appeareth! †
Yonder white rock, that the panting bird neareth,
Shelters a courser as fresh as the morning—
Rider and roan, for the race they are burning.

On like a whirlwind the wild hunter rushes,
Now, now, the plumes of the victim he brushes!
Too soon with triumph his dark eye is bright'ning!
Far, far before him she sweeps like the lightning!

---

* Shérb-el-Ríh, wind-drinker, is an epithet applied to the swiftest horses.

† The ostrich has very little cunning, never *doubles* in her flight, but depends on her speed alone, and runs in a straight course. Several horsemen post themselves at distances of about a league from each other on the line of flight; and when one stops, the next takes up the pursuit, and thus the bird is constantly chased by fresh horses. Of course the last horseman secures the prize.

Barb of the desert, thy breeding is noble,
Yet hope thou not, though thy mettle were double,
E'er to o'ertake the wing'd giant that races
Fast as the rack which the hurricane chases!

Once more from ambush a horseman outleapeth;
Thine, gallant gray, is the foot that outstrippeth
Samiel, the sun-born; now prove what thou darest;
On for the prize! 'tis thy master thou bearest!

Rapid, direct, as the ball when it flashes
Out through the smoke-wreath, the fiery Bey dashes
Forth on the game, that yet slacks not nor falters,
Right-ward or left-ward her course never alters.

Sky, air and earth in the noontide are seething,
Stifling and hot is the dust-cloud they're breathing,—
Little reck they of the shrivelling heaven,
Heed not the fire-shower that o'er them is driven!

Hour after hour the pursued and pursuing
Scour o'er the sand-waste, their speed still renewing;
Foam-mantled steed, how thy sobbing gasps thicken!
Bird of the Sahara, thy lagging steps quicken,

So art thou safe! 'Tis too late! lo, already
Trail her fringed wings, and her foot is unsteady!
Blindly she staggers, she seeketh to hide her!
Courage, bold gray, and thou soon art beside her!

Headlong she rolleth, still fluttering and shivering,
O'er her the courser stands panting and quivering,
Aali hath lifted his weapon, she boundeth
High in the death-throe, her flapping wing soundeth

Hoarse as the tempest; the frightened steed starteth,*
Swerves, plunges, rears, till the saddle-girth parteth;
Off springs his lord, down the barb droppeth dying,
Courser and camel-bird side by side lying!

* The victory is not without danger. The fluttering of the bird's wings, as she falls, inspires the horse with a sudden terror, which often proves fatal to the rider.

THE CHASE.

The chase is o'er, the fiery day
To night's cool splendors fast gives way.
Aali commands his weary train
To seek Sheikh Moosa's tents again;
There yesternoon the generous chief
To every want gave prompt relief,
And there the pacha will abide
Till the red flush of morning-tide.

Didst e'er those valleys green behold,
Of Desert Araby the pride,
By glowing hills encircled wide,
Like emeralds set in chiselled gold?
Didst ever there at evening lie
And watch, beneath a royal palm,
How the great moon came up the sky
In all her majesty of calm,
Yet shedding beams as bright as those
Shot from Prince Arthur's flaming shield,

When he unveiled it to his foes
And left them sightless on the field?
There hast thou heard, the livelong night,
The shrill cicala's quavering lay,—
She could not know such glorious light
Was not indeed the golden day!—
And hast thou marked the slender thread
Of crystal shining at thy feet,
Winding along its agate bed
With flow so soft, so silvery sweet,
While the lush oleander gazed,
By her own wondrous beauty dazed,
Into the watery mirror clear,
Where all her lovely blooms appear?
In such a vale Sheikh Moosa rests,
On such a night receives his guests.

Stately the welcome that he gave,
Such as became a patriarch grave.
"Be Allah's peace upon thy head!"

"Nor less on thine that peace be shed!"

"O Bey! lo, all that late was mine,
My flocks, my herds, my tents are thine!
The meanest slave that follows thee
Shall hunger not, nor thirst with me."

"O master of the tent!" replied
The Bey, "thy courtesy was tried
But late; our presence here to-night
Proves that we value it aright."

Then Aali to his tent repairs,
While for his guest Sheikh Moosa cares.
He bids his servants haste to bring
Fair water from the living spring,
So grateful to the traveller's feet
After such day of toil and heat.
Then smoking viands follow fast
And long, till milk and dates at last
Conclude the generous repast.

Tunisia's lord doth here abate
Somewhat of his accustomed state,
For he has learned that fiery blood
Of Bedouin brooks not haughty mood,
And willingly he would not know
A powerful desert chief his foe.
Now he demands with kindly air,
" How doth thy little warrior fare—
The boy that yesterday did ride
So proud and fearless by thy side,
And with his mimic martial play
Made every heart around him gay ? "

The sheikh replied, " At this late hour
He slumbers in his mother's bower;
But if my lord till dawn remain,
He shall behold the child again."

With the long day's rude pleasures spent,
On carpet soft the Bey now sleeps,

And ever round his princely tent
A faithful watch Sheikh Moosa keeps.
The azure field above it spread
Hangs not more silent overhead,
Than lies the little vale below
Till the dawn lifts her jewelled brow,
And bids the morning-star that waits
Throw wide the Orient's shining gates.
Then from his couch doth Aali start,
And give the signal to depart.

His morning orisons were o'er,
His chafing steed at the tent-door;
Leave of his host he turned to take,
And courteous were the words he spake;
Fair wishes many, thanks were none—
The Moslem thanks his God alone.

The sheikh made answer, "Hear, O Boy!
And for a moment yet delay.

Thou art my guest since yestereven,
And I, with Allah's aid, have striven
Our Prophet's precept to fulfil,
And keep thee from all pain and ill.
Such duty may not be discussed,
The guest is Allah's sacred trust.
If then the service of this night
Hath found acceptance in thy sight,
I pray thee with thy presence deign
To grace a mournful funeral train."
He paused, his pale lips trembled fast,
And through his frame a shudder passed.
Then calm resuming, "Know," he said,
"The child that won thy praise is dead!
The noonday sun shot through his brain
A deadly dart of mortal pain;
An hour before thy horses' tread
Sounded afar, his spirit fled.
So Allah willed it! Be it so!
Who but the all-knowing God should know

Whether we need or joy or woe!
But when thy train came up the vale,
I bade the women cease their wail—
Even the poor mother, wild with woe,
I charged her outcries to forego;
And to secure obedience, swore
That if one sob of hers my guest
Should reach, to trouble feast or rest,
Henceforth she was my wife no more!
Thou knowest, O Bey, if sound or sight
Of grief hath touched thy heart this night!
Then join thy faithful prayers with mine,
That on the dead God's face may shine!"

The Bey stood speechless as in trance,
Wonder and pity in his glance,
Then, " 'Tis the will of God!" he said,
And followed where Sheikh Moosa led.

Within the tent of grief they stand;
On a rich mat the fair child lies;

Circling him round in double band
The wailers rend the air with cries.
" Alas, for him ! " the mother moans,
" Alas, for him ! " a weeper groans,
" Alas, for him ! " in chorus wild
They shriek, " Alas, alas the child ! "
Calmly the sleeper sleeps the while,
And smiles great Azrael's heavenly smile.
They shower upon his marble breast
The costliest spices of the East;
Around the little form they wind
The richest broideries of Ind ;
Then raise the mat with tender care,
And forth the mournful burden bear.

Louder and shriller swells the wail ;
Wildly, in sign of heaviest bale,
The women toss their kerchiefs blue,
Then beat their breasts, their shrieks renew.

But hark! the Moolah strikes the chant!
The mourners cease their piercing plaint.
"Allah is great! His will be done!"—
So did the solemn chorus run—
"Allah is gracious, He doth give!
Is wise, He taketh when he will!
Good at His hand shall we receive,
And murmur when He sendeth ill?
Let for the child our sorrows cease!
May Allah keep his soul in peace!"

While thus of mingled prayer and praise
The measured hymn to Heaven they raise,
With regular but rapid tread
To his last rest they bear the dead.
Too long the parted soul doth wait
At the dark grave for her lost mate!
There the crushed bud with tearful rite
They hide forever from their sight.

Slowly and reverently the men
Turn backward to their tents again.
The women linger still to mourn;
"Moon of our darkness, Oh, return!
O fountain of our desert, why,
Why is thy spring thus early dry?
O fair young palm, why didst thou fade,
When we were sporting 'neath thy shade?
Why fall and crush us, cruel tree?
Did we not love thee tenderly,
Lead the sweet water to thy root,
That thou above all palms mightst shoot?
Thy mother why didst thou forsake,
And leave her wretched heart to break?"

Awhile the Moolah stands aloof,
Then mildly speaks a grave reproof;
"Ye women, trouble not the dead!
He hath not stood in Allah's stead
To fix the measure of his years!

Oh, dry your unavailing tears!
Let faith and prayer assuage your woes,
And leave the grave to its repose!"

Admonished thus, their grief they stayed,
And silent there a moment prayed,
Then with sad looks still backward cast,
Forth from the place of tombs they passed.

Meanwhile toward Nefta rode the Bey,
And on his heart strange burden lay.
Was it the morning's sight of woe
That left his sluggish pulse so low?
Aali was wont to look on death,
And lightly valued life's poor breath.
'Twas no weak terror of the tomb
That wrapped his spirit in this gloom.
It was the agony of life,
The change, the chance, the mortal strife,
That o'er the vision of his soul

Swept like the storm-cloud's onward roll,
Casting its heavy shadows broad,
Even o'er the path already trod
In smiling sunshine, till at last
In night lie future, present, past.
Haunts not as oft such darkening spell
The banquet as the burial?

The pacha strove to change his mood,
To see through all the evil good;
Yet ever at his heart there lay
A weight he could not roll away.
Forward he spurs—What fearful need
Doth urge yon horseman's headlong speed,
That toward him rides? Behold, they meet!
The messenger lies at his feet—
Hath rent his robe with gesture wild,
And on his head the dust hath piled.
"What are thy tidings? varlet, say!"
Exclaimed the darkly-frowning Bey.

"Alas, alas! O master mine.
And must I give to ears of thine
The tale I bring! This night accursed,
A storm of desert-robbers burst
Upon our guards, who bled in vain.
Thy gates are forced, thy servants slain.
Thy daughter—o'er the reeking dead
They leaped, and with their captive fled!"

CANTO IX.

THE ARRIVAL.

The sea of song and story, the sea that knows no tide!
How softly o'er its waters yon argosy doth ride!
Her path by fair Trinacria, that queen of islands, lies,
Where Ætna's smoke-wreathed forehead is lifted to the skies.
A breath, the mildest, steadiest of summer's' welcome gales,
Hath smoothed the rugged billows, and gently fans her sails.
No foam her bows are shedding; as noiseless doth she pass
As ship in realm of Faery, that glides o'er waves of glass.
Yet one her deck is pacing that marks with many a sigh
The amethyst of ocean, the azure of the sky.
His spirit, faint with longing, would hold it better far
To meet the black-winged storm-cloud, to mount its thundering car,

And homeward through the midnight with whirlwind-speed
    to ride,
'Twixt walls of leaping foam-flakes, red lightning for his
    guide!
Nor marvel at such choosing! his soul hath pined in chains,
Borne slavery's sharp anguish, its more than deathly pains
For years, till gold gave freedom—now swells his breast
    with joy,
To think how glad they'll greet him, their long lost island-
    boy,
With blessing, with caressing—Oh, here how shall he wait
For sluggish winds that loiter, and keels with fettering
    freight!
Long, long with foot impatient from stem to stern he strode,
Then, weary, o'er the bulwarks he leaned in peevish mood,
And bent his eyes, half conscious, upon the placid flood.

When rudely tossed by passion, thy heart has striven in vain
Through reason's sovereign mandate its quiet to regain,
When cares of life were rolling their wild and vapory rack

Around thee and above thee, and darkening all thy track—
Yet thou hast shrunk from praying, because thou wert ashamed
To call upon the Master, who surely must have blamed
Thy own weak faith full sharply ere He the tempest tamed.
Oh then, hast ever turned thee from warring thoughts within,
The fear, the hope, the longing, the struggle and the sin—
From these hast ever turned thee to look on Nature's face,
That still reflects so clearly her Author's constant grace?
She calms thee with her silence, she soothes thee with her sound,
And like a loving mother's her arms enfold thee round.
Then softly doth she whisper, " Go, erring child, go pray!
If haply so our Father forgive thy sin this day ! "
Great Angel of creation ! God placed thee at our side,
An ever present guardian to cheer us and to chide.
Thy glorious forehead blazing with stars of differing grace,
Thy wings of light outstretching through boundless fields of space,
Thy rainbow garments trailing along thy shining path,

Thy voice, now loving music, now terrible in wrath,
Thy mighty power to quicken the dullest human heart,
Declare from the beginning whose minister thou art!
Oh, still thy heavenly message of trust and patience speak
To all whose hearts are troubled, whose clouded faith is weak!

Now mark the restless stranger! as down the crystal wave
He looks, his pulse grows calmer, his anxious brow less grave.
What sees he there? A landscape, more bright, more strangely fair
Than ever yet hath gladdened the realms of upper air.
Over a briny ocean no longer doth he seem
Borne by a lifeless framework of canvas, bolt and beam,
But raised on spirit pinions through ether seas to go,
With the old heavens above him, and a new world below.
His brain swims as he gazes down many a fathom deep,
Where plain and hill and valley alternate past him sweep;
Broad shining plains all sparkling with rippled sands of gold,
O'erstrewn with gem-like pebbles and radiant shells untold;

Hills clothed with graceful forests or rough with jagged rocks,
Slopes purple as Hymettus, the wild thyme in his locks,
Or ledges steeply shelving, whence silken tangles fall
In broad and flowing fringes, as wrought for regal pall;
Valleys, where clustering thickets of crimson coral grow,
Where flowers the fair astrea white as the maybloom's snow.
With pearly tassels drooping, the actinia here is seen,
And there the crimpled sea-fan named of the foam-born queen;
Anemones and daisies and lilies scarcely blown,
Arrayed in robes of splendor are o'er those gardens strewn.
Not Jove's bloom-loving daughter e'er gathered buds so bright
Where Mongibello weareth his crown of flame by night.
Broad palm-like plumes are waving o'er beds of branching moss,
And polished sea-vines flaunting in mazy turnings cross,
Then twine in garlands braided with living buds and flowers,
Whose amaranthine beauty shames Flora's choicest bowers;

Crowns wrought of purest crystal, or woven of burning stains
As deep as ever kindled in old cathedral panes.
Well might the Tyrian's cunning draw forth, of ocean-birth,
A beam whose flaming lustre should pale the tints of earth!
Nor life nor motion lacketh that vision wondrous rare;
Moss, vine and wreath are swinging, as rocked by vernal air.
Forth from the coral copses the glossy fishes dart
In armor sheen enamelled beyond all power of art;
Now through the subtle fluid a single silvery flash
Shoots silent as a moonbeam, and now with muffled plash
In dazzling shoals they're flying, like flocks of timid doves,
That scared by stranger footsteps in clouds forsake the
    groves.
Medusas float in myriads, as light as mists of morn,
Which melting in the sunrise are up the valley borne;
Now stainless as the dew-drops that gem the grassy spires,
Now dyed with hues that rival the opal's changeful fires.
Aye, bring your brightest jewels, your stones of clearest ray
Before these ocean-glories their light will fade away!*

    * See Quatrefage's Souvenirs d'un Naturaliste.

Lost in o'erwhelming wonder the humbled youth exclaims;
"O Father, by the tenderest of all Thy chosen names,
By Thy great love incarnate, forgive my soul that still
Against Thine awful counsels hath raised a sinful will!"

  What feverish throb of life our isle
  Now stirs, that lay so calm erewhile?
  Why do they hurry to the shore,
  And send their searching glances o'er
  The roughening sea? What! know'st thou not,
  From Hamburg city news is brought,
  That Melleff, son of Amroom, late
  A slave in Barbary, doth wait
  In her safe port for wind and tide
  To waft him to our island's side?
  To-day the breeze blows fresh and fair,
  To-day the favoring tide rolls high,
  To-day no sea-mists blind the air,
  The bark that bears him must be nigh!
  The downs in panting haste they climb,

THE ARRIVAL.

The young, the old, the weak, the strong,
Even the poor widow of my rhyme
I miss not from the happy throng.
She gave her all to save the boy—
Should she not share the father's joy?

Ah me! the father! who may know
His heart, or knowing, think to show!
Silent he stands, as in a dream,
Apart upon his chosen knoll,
Within his eye no kindling beam,
But patience strong within his soul.
On his pale features none can trace
The cheer that gladdens every face
Save his. Yet is it strange that years
Of blasted hopes and freezing fears
Should rob him of the power to feel
Assurance strong of coming weal?
That one so long, so deeply sad
Forgets to smile, though he be glad?

'A sail? a sail?' the questioning word
In doubtful murmurs first is heard.
'A sail! a sail!' the shout breaks loud
And full from the rejoicing crowd.
Aye, there it shines! a point of light,
And now a little silvery thing,
As tiny as the sea-mew's wing
When seen afar in distant flight;
Now with a fuller pinion spread,
Higher it lifts its sun-lit head;
Onward the swelling cloud comes fast,
Filled with the freshening western blast.
Now mast and model fairly show,
Now the familiar flag they know.
Wolfe trembles. At his failing side
The pastor stands, and strives to hide
His own strong passion; words of cheer
He speaks; the old man doth not hear.
But ever nigher and more nigh
The bounding bark comes dancing on;

THE ARRIVAL.

Straight toward our isle her course doth lie.
Let every chilling doubt be gone!
The winding channel now she threads,
As one that well-known pathway treads,
And now at anchor doth she ride;
They lower a boat—with waving hand
A youth leaps down the vessel's side,
The oars pull swiftly toward the strand—
Distrustful father, fear no more!
Behold thy faith's long trial o'er!
Down every cheek the tears run warm,
And prayers gush forth from every soul,
As Wolfe, stayed by the pastor's arm,
With staggering step descends the knoll.
But ere his tottering feet can reach
The shore, the boat hath touched the beach.
The eager youth with one strong bound
Leaps to the land—looks anxious round.
Will no one greet him? wherefore stand
In such amaze that island band?

The old man's eye grows fixed and wild—
Oh God! 'tis not—'tis not his child!
Fainting he sinks with murmur low,
" My heart foretold the coming blow ;
Grant patience, Thou who seest my woe!"
Around the stricken sire they group,
O'er him with pitying look they stoop,
They lift his head upon their knees,
They bare his bosom to the breeze,
Chafe the stiff hand, and still anew
Wipe from his brow the chilling dew
Cold as the gathering damps of death,
Then listen for the silent breath.

Ah, hapless stranger! still alone
Dost stand, unwelcomed and unknown?
Is this the hour to which for years.
Thy soul hath looked through toil and tears?
Is this the hope that made thee strong
To bear the shame, the burning wrong?

THE ARRIVAL.

For this didst pray the lagging breeze
To speed thy bark across the seas?
Yet stay—thou art not all forgot!
Though other eyes may guess thee not,
Thy mother still doth know her son.
Yea, though thou come to her as one
Raised from the dead. Old Helda tries
To speak—but words her tongue denies.
Then, as if touched by charmed spell,
From off her bending shoulders fell
The weight of years, she stood upright,
Her eyes beamed with their earlier light;
Forward she sprang—now, now he knows
His mother—on her neck he falls,
Her widowed arms about him close,
And weeping, on his name she calls:
"Melleff! my son—or do I dream?
Art thou my child, or dost but seem?"
Aye, aye 'tis he, thou may'st believe
The lost is found, the dead doth live.

The shepherds' eyes are held no more,
They give him welcome o'er and o'er;
And now they ask how all befell;
And now the happy youth doth tell
That he, a slave in Tunis kept,
For years in bitter bondage wept,
Till sent from Amroom ransom came
For captive that should bear his name.
This burst his chains, and he hath come
To die upon his island home.
"And Melleff, son of Wolfe—hast brought
Tidings of him?" He knoweth nought,
Not even his captivity!
Old man, he brings no joy to thee!
The price sharp self-denial won
Redeemed a slave, but not thy son!*

---

* There are no family names among the Frisians, the patronymic Wolfson, Peterson, &c., serving to distinguish different individuals of the same Christian name. These names, too, are so few, that the same is borne by many, and of course such an accident as is described in the text, and is actually affirmed to have happened in the case narrated by Kohl, is by no means improbable.

CANTO X.

THE RESCUE.

Where heaven's arch of flaming ether
Sahara clasps in close embrace,
Till 'twixt upper fires and nether
Scarce the doubtful line you trace,
Mark yon lurid cloudlet swinging,
Rolling, eddying, thickening fast,
Broken sand-wreaths wildly flinging
Out upon the stifling blast!
Is it then the robe that drapeth
Samiel in its burning fold,
And which thus he madly shapeth
To his form of fearful mould?
Or the lightning's dread pavilion

Borne by fierce Euroclydon,
With its fringes dyed vermilion
In the blazing noonday sun?
Nay, not these? what then hath shaken
Such a sand-shower o'er the plain?
Flying steeds that do not slacken,
Steeds, whose riders draw not rein!
He that foremost sharply spurreth
Wears a front that hero fits;
Some great deed his spirit stirreth,
Triumph on his forehead sits!
On his arm a maid he stayeth,
And her eye is calm and clear,
And her queenly brow betrayeth
Not a doubt, and not a fear.
At his belt a sword is gleaming,
Scarlet stains his vesture mar,
Tides from many a gash are streaming,
Purple wounds his visage scar.
Close and sharp hath been the fighting;

Yea, for even the maiden's hand,
Suited ill for deadly smiting,
Grasps a short but blood-stained brand!
In the gest of that same maiden,
In that hand with blood defiled,
And with mortal weapon laden,
Canst thou see the pacha's child?
In that form of stately bearing,
In that look so proud and brave,
In that deed of highest daring,
Canst thou see the pacha's slave?
Tell me, to discern art able
Fleecy cloud of sheenest ray
In that band of awful sable
Where the linked lightnings play?
Dost thou know the quiet mountain
Where the humbled Titans sleep,
When red flame and fiery fountain
From the rent volcano leap?
So in gentle heart close hidden

Deep the electric current lies,
Till, by some strong passion bidden,
Forth the shattering levin flies !
So in manly heart, though breathing
Scarce 'neath mountain-weight of woe,
Boils a flood that yet with seething
Lava-tides may overflow !

'Twixt the midnight and the dawning,
Melleff heard the cry of fear
Mingled with the deathly groaning,
Tramp of steed and clash of spear.
' Was it thine, that shriek despairing,
Sheltering angel of my life ? '
Headlong then, like lion glaring,
Rushed he toward the sound of strife.
But too late ! amain they're flying
Through the moonlight with their prize—
Nought he meets save dead and dying,
And old Gerda with her cries.

In a breath behold him mounted,
Armed and dashing o'er the field,
With him horsemen ten, all counted
That might still a weapon wield.
Close the robber-tracks they follow,
Which the moon-rays still reveal,
And the earth rings deep and hollow
'Neath each flashing hoof of steel.
Now, brave Melleff, now God speed thee!
Chains and wrongs thou hast forgot!
She, thy guardian, she doth need thee,
Else thou dost remember nought!

Fast they ride till Phosphor waning
Drowns in Phœbus' jets of gold,
Fast they ride, and fast are gaining
On the wild marauders bold,
Who are thundering down the valley,
Through the palm-grove far and fast,
Till with maddening speed they sally

Out upon the desert waste.
Christian, let thy courage fail not!
Cheer thy feeble, fainting band!
Ere the noontide, if they quail not,
Yon proud sheikh shall bite the sand!
He hath marked his swift pursuer,
Noted every shining lance,
And behold! their number fewer
Than the third of those that glance
At his bidding! Lo, he turneth,
Stays his followers in their flight,
Bids them count the foe he spurneth,
And address them to the fight.

While the trembling girl he places
In a faithful vassal's care,
She hath seen where Melleff chases
Hotly through the quivering air.
She hath heard the fatal order:
"If, by chance thy chieftain fall,

Bear the maiden o'er the border
To Algeria's princely hall!"

Hark, the shock! the clang of weapons!
They have met—the battle cry
Rises shrill—the conflict deepens—
How they charge, they wheel, they fly,
Then return, the fight renewing,
With a fierce and frantic yell,
Thirsty sands with blood bedewing—
Men are they, or fiends of hell?

Fatmeh, see! now here, now yonder,
How the bright-haired Northman wheels!
Stroke on stroke like rattling thunder
With resistless arm he deals!
Count the lifted spears that quiver,
Aimed at breast of Christian foe—
Count the broken spears that shiver
'Neath his swifter, surer blow!

Now he fronts the bold Abdallah;
Fiery chief, how low he lies!
Furious shouts of Wallah! Wallah!
From his maddened followers rise.
Scathing flames of vengeance deaden
Memory to all other thought;
Even he who guards the maiden
Hath his latest charge forgot.
Fierce he spurs, and fast he speedeth
Toward the crimson battle-ring,
Nor the shuddering Fatmeh heedeth,
If she fall, or if she cling.
Yet she clung, she saw them pressing
On her wounded champion sore,
Saw assailants still increasing,
Saw his visage stained with gore!
Yet she clung! convulsive holding
Fast her warder's silken sash,
And within its ample folding
Sudden saw a dagger flash.

Ere his hand, already lifted,
Could at Melleff hurl the dart,
She, with new-born virtue gifted,
Plunged that dagger in his heart!
In a moment——but who showeth
How, in such a blinding fray,
Where scarce foeman foeman knoweth—
Safe on Melleff's arm she lay!
Wheeling then he swiftly darted
O'er the wild, like winged light,
And his little band, brave-hearted,
Covered well that headlong flight.
In that headlong flight behold them
Scorching sand-waves scouring o'er,
Though a backward glance hath told them
That the foe pursues no more.

See, alas! the fair head droopeth,
Faints with fasting and fatigue;
Yet the blasted waste still slopeth

Eastward far for many a league.
And not yet the charm is spoken
By the magi of the West,
Bidding crystal streams unbroken
Gush from out its arid breast.*
Fount refreshing, fruit-tree laden—
Vain it were to seek them here!
Must she perish, hapless maiden,
With a freedom bought so dear?

Melleff, through the air's hot glimmer
Mark'st thou not yon lowly dome,
With its white, its dazzling shimmer?
'Tis a holy Imaum's tomb!
Ishmael's sons, in death still yearning
As in life, make latest choice
Of the desert bare and burning,

---

* The French have bored a considerable number of Artesian wells in the Algerine Sahara, and similar operations have been carried on within a few years in Egypt, and other parts of Northern Africa. See an interesting article in the Revue de l'Orient, for September, 1858.

THE RESCUE.

Where God heard their father's voice.
To the sacred precincts hasten!
There, in memory of the dead
Whose pure life was but this lesson :
' Help thy brother in his need '—
Pious hands for desert ranger
Store have left of choicest fruit,
And to bless the thirsty stranger
Bared the spring to its deep root.*
Thither Melleff anxious flieth,
And beneath the welcome shade
Which the narrow dome supplieth,
Softly lays the unconscious maid ;
Then in trembling haste he bringeth
Water from the scanty well,
And the cooling drops he flingeth
O'er her, wake her like a spell.
Starting up, she names her father—
"Gerda, why hast left me so?"

* See Appendix IX.

And, as one who dreameth rather,
Closely clasps her throbbing brow.

Oh, 'twere pity to behold her
Pale as Cynthia's struggling ray,
While the fever-mists enfold her
That she strives to chase away!
Richer gifts of form and feature
Ne'er did mortal maiden share,
And to Melleff mortal creature
Never shone so heavenly fair.
He would die the doubt to banish
That with darkness fills her brain—
Lo, the passing shadows vanish,
And her eye is clear again!

" Aye, I know—yet why delay we?
My deliverer, wherefore wait?
Nefta's bowers lie far—why stay we?
And my father's grief is great!"

"Princess, let no doubt affray thee!
We but sought a moment's rest;
Take this draught, this fruit, I pray thee,
And we ride at thy behest."

Hurriedly the cup she draineth—
What new tidings of dismay
Brings the watchman, that constraineth
Melleff even to blanch away?
They have seen the dust-cloud rising,
Steely lightnings flash it through!
Is its tawny mask disguising
Welcome friend or dreaded foe?
Shall they fly, or shall they tarry
Till the painful doubt be clear?
How the fickle judgments vary!
Now they hope and now they fear.
With such burden wer't not better
Friend to miss than foe to meet?

In the saddle they have set her,
Off they dash at furious heat.

Gallant heart! was never braver
On a noble purpose bent.
But, alas! thou canst not save her,
For thy flagging steed is spent.
Vain the spurring, the caressing!
Like the fire-wave's rolling flow,
On thy track that cloud is pressing—
Thou must turn and face the foe!
Foe—but stay! whose pennon streameth
High above the smothering haze?
Whose the armor bright that beameth
Forth with such a ruddy blaze?
Now, be praise to Him that saveth!
For the right He doth decide.
There Tunisia's banner waveth,
There her noble lord doth ride!

How they send their shouts to heaven,

Shouts of triumph and of cheer,

When, as by a whirlwind driven,

Aali with his train sweeps near

CANTO XI.

THE VISION.

The night-lamp's feeble flame burns low,
The trembling stars are looking through
The checkered lattice, and their light
Drops on the marble flooring bright
As Luna's beam on Northern night.
No flaunting silks, no stifling panes
Of crystal, or of varied stains,
Obstruct the broken rays that fall
In silver fretwork on the wall,
Where pearl with tortoise-shell combines
In a mosaic chaste and rare,
Bordered with wreaths of golden vines,
That seem outfloating on the air.

But gilded roof and arch are lost
In shadows that no star hath crossed.
A trickling fountain's lulling flow
Unseen doth greet the listener's ear,
While fannings of faint sweetness show
The lily and the rose are near;
And there its drapery's glossy shine
Alone the silken couch betrays,
Where the pale Fatmeh doth recline,
O'er whom in silence Gerda prays.
For days hath frenzied fever laid
His fiery hand upon her head,
With phantoms dire her brain possessed,
And filled her soul with dark unrest.
The shadow of death's wing is nigh;
Oh, will he smite her, or pass by?

At length the leaping pulses flow
More calmly; since the midnight hours
She softly sleeps; her breathing now

Is soundless as the breath of flowers.
In the old nurse there stirreth naught
Save the swift lightning of her thought,
That knows a readier path to find
To the far land that gave her birth,
Than through the electric links that bind
So close the once dissevered earth;
For she hath fasted, prayed and wept,
Till the soul's vision, that had slept
Somewhat from age, now backward cast,
In one broad glance holds all the past.

No more a weak and withered thing,
Wasted by time and tears, she seems,
But a young wife, whose fresh glad spring
Is opening in love's sunniest beams.
Again on Iceland's rocky coast
She sits beneath the pole-star's ray,
Its pale, calm shining well nigh lost
In the wild North-light's dancing play;

Again her childish fancy paints
Those silvery flashes as the light
Left by the wings of blessed saints,
Who take to God their happy flight.
Far to the east stands Hecla, crowned
With roaring flame, and girt around
With everlasting icy chains,
Outpouring from his lava-veins
Rivers of fire, that red and wide
Are rolling down his snow-clad side.
The boiling Geysers thundering shoot
From seething fountains vast as seas
That lie beneath his burning foot,
And swing their arms upon the breeze,
Like giant palms of crystal, wrought
Till light as from Arachne caught.
Of the old landscape, oh, how clear
Each sight and sound strikes eye and ear!
And yet the midnight sun hath cast
For fifty years his annual smile

Upon the snow-peaks of that isle
Since she hath looked upon it last.
Looked last! she shudders; fatal sight!
Let Lethe's mighty waters roll
Over the memory of that night,
And wash it from her troubled soul.
But no! that image cannot fade,
'Tis drawn in blood upon her heart,
Its crimson lines too deep inlaid
To pale till soul and body part;—
The midnight yell, the bolt's sharp crash,
The turbaned corsair's demon eyes,
The crescent-cimetar's keen flash
'Neath which her murdered father lies,
Her shrieking infant wrenched away
From her and cast to earth like clay,
The cries of the resisting band
Led down despairing to the sea,
The death-strokes dealt by Olaf's hand,
His groan of hopeless agony,

When bleeding, dying, on the shore
He lay, while hellish pirates bore
His Gerda to their bark accursed—*
These sights, these sounds of woe now burst
Upon her senses with a power,
A weight of horror, scarcely less
Than in the first o'erwhelming hour
That sealed her doom of wretchedness.
Again the sea's deep moan she hears,
Unmeaning words are in her ears,
And now a fellow-captive's wail
Is mingled with the sobbing gale.

Yet are these memories more dim;
Soon as the crushing blow was dealt,
Over her soul strange stupor came,
The broken heart but little felt.
That voyage of months—it fills no space
On the broad tablet of her thought—

* See Appendix X.

A blackness that revealeth naught,
A point alone that hath but place.
But when they reached the hateful shore,
Then was the unconscious respite o'er,
Then did her tortured bosom swell
With anguish wild, unutterable.
The market-place—O Gerda! why
Wilt thou recall that agony?
Nay, pass it o'er! pass all those years
When day and night thy meat was tears—
Pass onward to the better hour
That freed thee from a tyrant's power,
And placed thee in young Maani's bower!
There gentle pity didst thou find
With her, the generous, true and kind.
Sweet Maani! through the Orient famed,
The fairest rose that e'er had birth
In far Circassia, meetly named
Mother of beauty for the earth—
Alas! not hope that smiled before her,

THE VISION.

Not all the love that Aali bore her,
Not the dear infant on her heart,
Could save her from the icy dart
Of Death, whom grief, reproach and prayer
Alike have striven to move in vain,
Since the first hour of his dark reign,
The loveliest and the best to spare.
From all that joy in life could waken
Was the blest wife and mother taken—
And *she*, of every pleasure reft,
The wretched, hopeless captive left.
And yet—how strange! the orphan child
Turned first to that despairing face,
And with a baby's matchless grace
Stretched forth its little arms and smiled.

Since then for Fatmeh hath she not
Felt all a mother's heart could feel,
And in that love nigh half forgot
Herself a slave, an exile still?

Now must she lose her? will she die?
Old dame, the cruel thought forbear—
'Twill slay thee; turn again to prayer;
God will not leave thee utterly!
She stirs, she speaks, thy foster-child—
Listen if still her words be wild!

"Gerda! art here? Oh, I have seen
A vision of such bliss to-night,
A glory so exceeding bright,
God's paradise it must have been.
I saw His blessed angels there,
Saints crowned with immortality,
I saw my mother wondrous fair,
And knew her, though none showed it me.
Into her opening arms I flew,
And on her soft and loving breast
She rocked me to a sweeter rest
Than ever weary childhood knew.
It was not sleep, for I could see

THE VISION.

The glory still that circled me,
And I could hear from golden lyres,
Swept by the hand of seraph-choirs,
Harmonious ravishment that thrilled
Beyond the power of song, that filled
My being to its utmost core
With rapture all undreamed before,
And in my soul sweet longings stirred
To be but one with what I heard.
It was not sleep! and yet I saw
Not all those heavenly eyes discerned—
I knew it by the holy awe
That through their milder meanings burned;
The majesty reflected there
Was all that mortal sight could bear

Then one drew near with floating tread;
I knew her straightway; it was she,
Who in the garden of the dead
Near Tunis, by the sounding sea,

WOLFE OF THE KNOLL.

Doth sleep—the princess Moonkir bore
From Frankistan's remotest shore,
And gave a rest so long, so calm,
On the blest shore of El-Islam,
Beneath the aloe, by the side
Of him for whom she meekly died.
And very meek the smile that lay
Upon her lips, as it would say,
' Less worthy I the crown of light
Than these who fought a better fight.'
" Sister," she said—and her tones fell
So softly that I cannot tell
If it were sound—" Oh, learn of me,
'Tis well to keep thy verity!
A holier cause than earthly love
Alone a maiden's heart should move
To leave her father and her faith.
Yet know, 'tis higher, greater far,
To live and conquer in such war
Than cowardly to call on Death.

Die unto self! aye, nobly slay,
With Allah's aid, that birth of sin
Which eats thy budding wings away,
And, grub-like, leaves but dust within.
Then live to God for man, till He
Take thee to His eternity!"
The vision passed while yet she spoke,
And full of joy and peace I woke.
Gerda, 'tis not the moment now,
Had I the power, to tell thee how
My heart hath tempted me to fly
With Melleff, or, renouncing, die!
Enough—at length my heaven-taught soul
Pants high for a diviner goal—
Is strong to take the longest road,
The roughest, mortal ever trod,
So it but lead at last to God—
To lose for earth one single beam
That crowned the pure immortal day
Beheld in my departed dream,

Were price too heavy far to pay.
Life's passing ills no more I blame,
E'en sorrow scarce deserves a name,
So brief her honr. Oh nurse, I know,
This thou hadst taught me long ago,
But happy youth will learn but slow!
Now my first prayer, 'let others see,
Father, what thou hast shown to me,'
And for myself but this alone,
The first, the last, ' Thy will be done!'
One work accomplished, then am I
Alike content to live or die."

She ceased, and fainting sank away
More wan than the first daylight ray
That full upon her forehead lay.
The trembling Gerda hastes to shed
The spicy waters on her head,
Throws back the mantling cloud of hair,
And bathes her in the morning air.

At last, the deathly weakness o'er,
She lifts her languid lids once more.

"Where is my father? doth he wake?"

"Aye, child and long, for thy dear sake."

"Then pray him, of his love, come near,
For I would speak what he should hear."

The pacha stood beside her bed,
The tears that manhood shames to shed
Pressed back, and, stooping calm and slow,
Kissed tenderly her ivory brow.
"Father, my feet have stood to-nigh,
Within the very gates of light!
Such grace hath Allah shown to me
That I am bold to sue to thee.
Then, for my mother's sake and mine—

Nay, rather, that God's face may shine
On thee when thou shalt stand alone
For judgment at his awful throne—*
Oh, set thy Christian captives free,
And send them safely o'er the sea!
What Melleff's hand for me hath wrought
This grace from thee hath nobly bought.
Grant but my prayer—duty and love
What else I cannot speak, shall prove!"

Again she swoons! how like to death!
No fluttering throb, no faintest breath
That marble stirs! Oh, was she taught
To live a true, great life for naught?
For naught! is this thy wisdom's reach?
That lesson deeply learned, what more
Doth the immortal on the shore
Of time, which can no further teach?

---

* All shall appear at the judgment, and every man alone. Koran.

The father with a heay groan
Turns from his child. With a low moan
Upon her neck falls Gerda—nay,
Now lift her not! 'tis clay to clay!

CANTO XII.

THE RETURN.

On the mainland stood the sun,
Looking westward o'er the water,
Till its glassy surface shone,
Crimson as a field of slaughter.
Wrapped in lightest autumn-haze
Amroom rested on the ocean,
Whose broad breast had heaved for days
Only with a tidal motion.
Not a breeze, in cloudy car,
O'er the morning sky was sweeping;
Hushed, all nature, near and far,
Lay as in the calmest sleeping.
Shepherds, silent as the scene,

Down their steepy hillocks wended,
And to pastures paly green,
With their eager flocks, descended.
Why so gravely toward the sea—
Each as neighbor neighbor passes—
Point they, though upon the lea
Not a zephyr stirs the grasses?
Do their quicker senses hear
Aught that may the storm betoken?
To the sod now lay thine ear—
Lo, the charmed silence broken! *
First by low and tender moans,
As of music that complaineth,
Then by deep and heavy groans,
As when anguish strong constraineth.
Now, as if the south wind passed
Through the pine-tree softly, sadly,
Now, as if the whirlwind's blast
Smote the forest fiercely, madly.

* See Appendix XI.

Nearer now, and yet more loud,
As when voiced lightnings quiver
Through the black tornado-cloud,
And the reeling cedars shiver.
'Tis the far-off chariot roll
Of the west wind, wildly speeding
Onward to its unseen goal,
Man and his poor works unheeding.
Woe to him whose careless sail
On the tempest's track is flying!
Fathom-deep, ere daylight fail,
Shall that hapless bark be lying.
Though for hours these waters sleep
Calm as lake in sheltering mountains,
While afar the mighty deep
Rolls upbroken to its fountains,
Yet round Amroom, isle of storms,
Shadows ere the sunset hover;
Night and cloud, their dusky forms
Mingling, soon its face will cover.

THE RETURN.

Howling winds blow high and cold;
Fast the shrouding darkness thickens;
Safe to house his shivering fold
Now his step the shepherd quickens.
Haste to aid him, wife and child!
Lest, before the work be ended,
Sky and shore and ocean wild
In one midnight deep be blended!

All are sheltered; thanking God,
Round their scanty fire they gather,
Calm they sit, as if abroad
Shone the softest, sunniest weather.
Not a glance of fear they cast
At the hissing waters round them,
Though the billow and the blast
Rise as if no fetter bound them.
Trusting in their Father's care,
Who will leave not nor forsake them,

With a short and childlike prayer
They to needful rest betake them.

Through the tempest's troubled roll
Is there then no eye but sleepeth?
Aye! for still upon the knoll
Wolfe his patient vigil keepeth!
Even that last, that cruel blow,
His unbroken faith surviveth,
Saying still, with Job, 'I know
Surely my Redeemer liveth!'
When from that long swoon he woke,
Straight to Heaven did he address him,
And the first faint words he spoke—
'Though He slay me I will bless Him'—
Scarce his shrunken lips had passed,
When the postman's bark came flying
O'er the cold gray waters fast
Toward the beach where he was lying.
Man of sorrow, lift thy head!

Comfort to thy heart it bringeth,
Hope, whose very root seemed dead,
Into sudden freshness springeth!
Letters in his hand they placed—
Letters, and his son doth send them!
Those clear lines so boldly traced,
Who but Melleff's self had penned them?
' He was free, on Christian land,
Hurriedly was homeward pressing,
And should reach their island-strand
Ere the winter, with God's blessing!'

From that hour Wolfe standeth strong,
Cloudless peace his soul possesses;
Though the waiting hath been long,
Not a doubt his heart distresses.
Day by day and week by week,
From the dawning until even,
Still he gazes, childly meek,
Seaward now, and now toward Heaven.

And to-night, though winds are high,
Friends in vain to rest entreat him;
"Sure," he saith, "my son is nigh,
And I must be here to greet him!"

Hark! the tide's advancing roar;
Shepherds, brief will be your sleeping!
Wave rolls wave against the shore,
Each in scorn the last o'erleaping.
Now the trembling mounds they smite,
Close around their bases curling;
O'er the roofs with doubling might
Briny flakes they now are hurling!
Cynthia, through the wind-rent cloud
O'er her rising glory drifted,
Sees above the foamy shroud
Cot and down alone uplifted.
How the cabins heave and rock
On the feathery crested surges,
While each quick returning shock

Half the dripping thatch submerges!
Breaking faintly through the gloom,
Lo, the feeble taper gleameth,
Flieth fast from room to room,
Through each narrow casement streameth!
They would save their household store—
Hurriedly aloft they bear it,
Pile it high above the floor,
So perchance the flood may spare it!
Silent then, with awe-struck look,
Close they press, while o'er them dashes
Wave on wave, with thundering shock,
And, beneath, the frail shed crashes.

Where is Wolfe? upon the down
Still he stands with soul unshaken;
Ocean's rage, the sky's wild frown,
Not a thought of fear can waken.
Cloven billows, higher, higher,
Round his pigmy isle are springing;

Darting up like tongues of fire,
To his very feet they're clinging!
Yet he heeds them not; his eye
Through the blinding night he straineth
Toward the perilous road, where lie
Ships, when stormy darkness reigneth.
Lo, through folded clouds the moon
With her silvery arrow pierces,
For a moment glances down,
And the thickest gloom disperses.
Some dark shape upon the tide,
Heaving slow, his vision fancies,
While along its blackened side
Light and free the sea-foam dances.
Dreamer, mocked for many a year,
Oft the broken reed hath thrust thee!
Schooled so sternly, dost thou dare
On a hope so frail to trust thee?
Yea! and through that awful night
With this hope his heart o'erfloweth,

Joyfully expects the light,
That the vessel surely showeth.
Fond old man, alas for thee!
Other sight thine eyes awaiteth
When the troops of darkness flee,
And the angry flood abateth!

Now spent ocean seeks his bed;
Morning in the orient lightens,
Robes the flying clouds with red,
And the weeping islet brightens.
Watcher, turn thee toward thy cot!
Lo, the angel that destroyeth,
Save thy life, hath left thee naught,
All in hopeless ruin lieth.
On the turfless, crumbling mound
Scarce an upright pile remaineth,
While the shapeless wreck around
Even the hungry sea disdaineth.
There the pitying neighbors throng,

Crying, "Hath our God forsaken
One that hath been tried so long?
Let his loving kindness waken!"

Brave old man! that sight the while
Stirs in him no strong emotion,
But again with chastened smile
Turns he to the throbbing ocean.
There she lies, a noble ship!
And the tempest hath not scathed her,
Though her shrouds and canvas drip
With the drenching floods that bathed her!
Springing from its perch, a bark
Wide its snowy wings outstretches,
Flies, like arrow to the mark,
Isle-ward till the shore it reaches.
Lo, he comes! and faith hath won
Her reward that faileth never.
"Now it is enough, my son!
Blessed be His name forever!"

THE RETURN.

Ye that, for love of the lowly, so long
Have patiently followed my simple song,
Do ye plain the lot of our Melleff still,
Though free over Amroom he walks at will?
Then ye know not how dear, if loved from birth,
The dreariest sod of a sin-cursed earth!
Ye know not the bondman's bitter estate,
The soul's keen joy with new freedom elate;
Ye know not how sweet on a father's head
The oil of gladness unmeasured to shed,
To purple his sunset with purer dye
Than ever had flushed in his morning sky!
Ye know not 'tis blesseder far to see
The idol we worship stretch suddenly
The wings of its glory, and fill the place
With brightness that proveth its heavenly race—
Though at last it soar, in its shining flight,
Too high to be followed by mortal sight—
Oh, blesseder far, than our incense to waste
On what but seems with divinity graced,

To kneel for long years, and cast at its feet
Our heart's best gifts as an offering meet—
Yet the altar still cold, nor voice nor sign
Proclaim the fair image indeed divine—
To see its proud colors fade day by day,
Its faultless lines crumble slowly away,
Till we find, at last, 'tis but common clay!

APPENDIX TO WOLFE OF THE KNOLL.

I.

For a mightie great compasse, their countrey lieth so under the Ocean, and subject to the tide, that twice in a day & night by turnes, the sea overfloweth a mightie deale of ground when it is floud, & leaveth all drie again at the ebbe & return of the water: insomuch, as a man can hardly tell what to make of the outward face of the earth in those parts, so doubtfull it is between sea and land. The poore sillie people that inhabit those parts, either keepe together on such high hils as Nature hath afforded here & there in the plain: or els raise mounts with their owne labour and handie worke (like to tribunals cast up and reared with turfe, in a campe) above the height of the sea, at any Spring tide when the floud is highest; and thereupon they set their cabines and cottages. Thus dwelling as they doe, they seeme (when it is high water, and that all the plaine is overspread with the sea round about) as if they were in little barkes floting in the middest of the sea: againe, at a low water when the sea is gone, looke upon them, you would take them for such as had suffered shipwracke, having their vessels cast away, and left lying ato-side amid the sands: for yee shall see the poore wretches fishing about their cottages, and following after the fishes as they go away with the water. They have not a four-footed beast among them: neither enjoy they any benefite of milke, as their neighbour nations doe: nay, they are destitute of all meanes to chase wild beasts, and hunt for venison; in as much as there is neither tree nor bush to give them harbour, nor any weare unto them by a great way. Sea-weeds or Reike, rushes and reeds growing upon the washes and meeres, serve them to twist for cords to make their fishing nets with. These poore soules and sillie creatures are faine to gather a slimie kind of fattie mud or oase, with their very hands, which they drie against the wind rather than the Sunne; and with that earth, for want of other fewell, they make fire to seeth their meat (such as it is) and heat the inward parts of their bodie, readie to be starke and stiffe againe with the chilling North wind. No other drinke have they but raine water, which they save in certaine ditches after a shower, and those they dig at the very entrie of their cottages. And yet see! this people (as wretched and miserable a case as they bee in) if they were subdued at this day by the people of Rome, would say (and none sooner than they) that they lived in slaverie. Pliny, Natural History, Book XVI. Chap. I.

II.

The ambassadors Verritus and Maloriges (in Frisic probably Freddens und Malrichsen) were complimented by an invitation to the theatre of Pompey, to witness a public entertainment. Being regarded as rustics, or rather semi-barbarians, they were not conducted to the box reserved for the imperial and royal diplomatic circle, but shown to seats in the second tier. Enquiring of their valet de place who the dignitaries were in the conspicuous lodge occupied by the foreign ministers, they were told that these were their Excellencies, the ambassadors from the kings and the great nations of the earth. Upon this, they exclaimed, "Na worum schält wi denn do nich sitten? Sin wir Freschen denn nich eben so god as de anuern? Wät ji Römers nich, det de Dütschen bäter upkloppen känt, un mehr Trü un Globen häft as de alle tosomen!" which Tacitus expresses in a very pompous, Italian, and un-Frisic way: "nullos mortalium armis aut fide ante Germanos esse." They now made their way, without ceremony, to the diplomatic box, and took their seats with the other ambassadors, which, as Tacitus says, was well received, as a sample of primitive spirit, "comiter a visentibus exceptum quasi impetus antiqui." Kohl, Vol. II, p. 325.

III.

Water is usually distributed to private houses in the east by carriers provided with goat-skins holding seven or eight gallons. These are filled at public fountains erected by the charity of the rich, and the water is sold in the streets, and very generally given freely to the poor.

"I was one day sitting," says Prax, "at the door of a coffee-house, when a boy came up with a full water-skin. He cried, 'Whosoever shall give four *nasseri* (one cent and a half) to relieve the thirst of the poor, shall see the mercy of God upon himself and his ancestors!' I gave him the four *nasseri*, and drank from a cup presented me by the sakka. He then offered the water to all comers, crying, 'O ye that are athirst! behold water given for the love of God! May the donor of this water see the mercy of God shed abroad upon his fathers.'" Revue de l'Orient, November, 1849.

IV.

The Prophet is traditionally reported to have said: Upon him who is hospitable God will bestow twenty gifts:

Wisdom;
A sure word;
The fear of God;
A heart always glad;
He shall hate none;
He shall not be proud;
He shall not be jealous;
Sadness shall flee away from him;
He shall hospitably receive all;
He shall be beloved of all;
He shall be respected, though he be of humble birth;
His goods shall be increased;
His life shall be blessed;
He shall be patient;
He shall be discreet;
He shall be always contented;

He shall care little for the good things of this world;
If he stumbles, God shall uphold him;
His sins shall be forgiven him;
And, finally, God shall preserve him from the evil which may fall from the heavens or rise from the earth.

Be generous to thy guest, for he cometh to thee with his good: when he entereth in, he bringeth thee a blessing; and when he departeth, he carrieth away thy sins.

V.

A Hallig preacher described to me his arrival in his parish much as follows:

"My reception was very touching," said he, hardly able to repress his tears. "How so, pastor?" asked I. "Well, I came down the geest (the mainland) with my wife, in a heavily-loaded waggon, for we had, besides our clothing, many things that good friends here and there had given us, to help our housekeeping on the Hallig. We reached the shore a day later than we expected, and found the boat that had been sent over for us lying by the dike. The poor people had waited two days, and had uncomfortable quarters in the mean time. They welcomed us, took our baggage on board, and we shoved off. We soon approached a waste, treeless island, and I asked the men if that was their Hallig. They took off their hats, and answered, 'Yes, pastor,' and I turned to my wife, and said, 'There, my child, that is the island where we are to live!' When we landed on the Hallig, we found the whole congregation assembled, men, women, and the children too, which much affected me. 'Did some one of the committee or the elders make a formal speech to you?' asked I. 'Oh no, not that.' 'Did the women and girls sing a song of welcome?' 'Oh, no; these good people never sing but in church.' I got out of the boat, helped my wife out, and said to them, 'Good morning, my dear children! I have brought you your pastor and pastoress. God bless you!' 'Did the girls scatter flowers before you, or bring you wreaths?' 'Oh, no, they have no flowers.' The men all came and pressed my hand in silence, and the women caressed us, and patting our shoulders, said, 'Good pastor and dear pastoress! It is very kind of you to be willing to be our pastor and pastoress!' And then they gathered up our boxes and bundles, each one taking a parcel, and led us to our house, which they had nicely swept and aired. The old men whispered to me that I need not fear for my salary, for they had collected it, and were ready to pay the whole sixty thalers* in advance. Then they showed me my garden-plot, and the church, which had also been swept. 'Had they dressed it with green branches?' 'Oh, no, they have neither branches nor trees, but they had hoisted a flag, which was waving in the wind, as they do on all festive occasions.' Many of them were affected to tears, and my wife and I could not control our emotion." Kohl, I. 349.

VI.

The usual period of leaving the islands (to engage in foreign maritime service) is St. Peter's day, which falls on the 29th of June. Many small vessels are freighted with mariners bound for the ports of Holland, and the wives, mothers, sisters, and sweethearts of the departing sailors assemble to bid them adieu. They gather upon an old heathen funeral mound in the island of Föhr, in their antiquated and picturesque costumes, accompanied by children and superannuated mariners, and make farewell signals from shore to ship, and from ship to shore, as long as they remain in sight of each other. St. Peter's day is also the general business day of the island. Old debts are paid, new ones incurred, and especially matrimonial engagements contracted, so that it is at once the most important epoch of the year, and an anniversary around which many of the most painful as well as tender and hopeful associations cling. Kohl, Vol. I. p. 155.

VII.

Amber is found in considerable quantities on the coasts of Schleswig-Holstein, the neighboring islands, and Jutland, as well as on the southern shores of the Baltic. It is thrown up on the beach by tempestuous

---

* Sixty thalers, or about forty-five dollars, is the annual salary of a Hallig pastor

weather, and sometimes on strands where the rise of the tide is so rapid that the gatherers of amber find it necessary to seek for it on horseback, in order to be able to escape from the returning flood. A single piece sometimes sells for several hundred dollars, but success in the search is so uncertain that it is, upon the whole, an unprofitable occupation.

In one of the North-Frisian dialects, amber is called *glæs*, a name known to none of the Germanic family, but which is evidently identical with the *glesum* of Tacitus (whence also the appellation Insulæ Glessariæ, or amber-islands.) Sed et mare scrutantur, ac soli omnium succinum, quod ipsi *glesum* vocant, inter vada atque in ipso litore, legunt. Tacitus de Germania, XLV. Kohl, Vol. III. p. 245.

According to an Arabian traveller of the tenth century cited by Ritter, Erdkunde, XIII. 749, the camels of Hadhramaut were employed in seeking amber upon the coasts of the Red Sea, being taught to kneel when they saw it glitter in the moonshine.

VIII.

The sand was drifting up day and night, and it was found impossible to make the windows and doors tight enough to exclude it, nor did it avail to shovel out the perpetually renewed incumbrance. Too poor to build a new church, the people continued to occupy this as long as possible.

The floor, and then the pews, were covered, the pulpit itself half buried in sand, and the congregation were seated upon the sand around it. At last the church was so nearly filled up that they could barely creep in at a window.

Divine service was now held in the church for the last time, the congregation broken up, and the building sold.

The purchaser employed such of the wood as he could save, in constructing a house, reserving the altar and the pulpit for finishing the cabin of his ship. On what far coast the vessel with her consecrated cabin-furniture was stranded at last, none could say. Kohl, Vol. II. p. 157.

IX.

Sidi-Mohammed-el-Gandouz, who lived, died and was buried on the spot where the piety of the faithful has since raised the marabout or funeral-chapel which bears his name, was renowned for the hospitality which travellers and the poor received from him.

Passing caravans aided his charities by leaving with him dried meats, flour, dates, butter, &c., which he distributed among the poor, whose supplies were exhausted, and the indigent pilgrims who came to visit him and pray with him. The practice has been kept up since his decease. No caravan passes his tomb without stopping to pray and leave a donation. All comers are allowed to enter the chapel, eat their fill, and satisfy their thirst; but woe to him who should carry any thing away! He would surely perish on his journey. There is none to watch the offerings, but there is no instance of the abuse of this 'hospitality of God.'

Charity, saith the Prophet, extinguishes sin, as water quencheth fire. It closeth seventy gates of evil.

An angel standeth at the gates of Paradise, crying; "Whosoever giveth alms to-day, shall be filled to-morrow." Daumas, l'Algérie. 95,

X.

In the year 1627, four Barbary corsairs visited various points of the coast of Iceland, plundered or destroyed churches, houses, and other property, killed thirty or forty of the natives, and carried off three hundred and fifty captives, among whom were two clergymen, with their families. Several causes, among which the principal was the treachery of persons who were intrusted with means to ransom them, prevented their release until 1635.

Some of them having become renegades, and many having died or been sold into distant slavery, only thirty-seven were found, and of these but thirteen lived to regain their native land. A brief notice of these occurrences will be found in Finn Jonsen's Hist. Eccl. Islandiæ, Vol. III. p. 83, and more particular narratives were published by Olaf Egilsson, one of the captives, by Klas Eyolfsson and by Björn á Skardsá

XI.

Our guide drew our attention to a roaring sound proceeding from the sea, which he said indicated a change of wind, and the approach of a storm. We heard a distant noise, which was more distinctly perceptible on applying the ear to the ground on the flats. Near us all was still, and as far as we could see, the finest weather. But in the far distance, there was a roaring and raging, as if all nature was in commotion. We could hardly imagine that it proceeded merely from the concussion of drops of water, and bubbles of foam. It sounded as if beams of wood were tumbling over each other, and shattering to splinters, and often there were harsh and clearly defined noises, as if a heap of cannon balls or rocks were rolling down a mountain. The sounds indeed were not so loud as when near at hand, but they were sharper, more rattling and crashing, so that it seemed scarcely possible that water could produce them. Kohl, II. p. 27.

POEMS.

POEMS.

NIÖRTHR AND SKATHI.

The third god [after Odin] is he who is named Niörthr; he dwells in heaven, where it is called Nóatún; he rules the going of the wind, and stills the sea and the fire; on him should men call in seafaring and fishing. He is so rich and lucky, that he can give to those who ask him much land or loose-goods. * * * * Niörthr has a wife named Skathi, the daughter of the giant Thiassi. Skathi would occupy the dwelling-place of her father; it is on certain fells, where it is called Thrumheimr; but Niörthr would live by the sea. They agreed to this; that they would stay nine nights at Thrumheimr, and then other nine at Nóatún. And when Niörthr came back to Nóatún from the fell, he chanted this:

    Leið erumk fjöll,   Tired am I of the fell,
    varka ek lengi,   I was not long there,
    nætr einar ix.;   Nine nights only;
    úlfa þytr   The wolves' howling
    mèr þótti illr vera   Seemed to me ill,
    hjá söngvi svana.   To the song of the swans.

Then Skathi chanted this:

    Sofa ek máttat   Sleep I could not
    sæfar beðjum á   On the sea shore
    fugls jarmi fyrir;   For the screaming of the birds;
    sá mik vekr,   He wakes me,
    er af viði kemr,   That comes from the sea,
    morgun hverjan már.   The mew, every morning.

Then Skathi went up to the fells, and dwelt in Thrumheim. She runs much on snow-shoes, carries a bow, and shoots wild animals; she is styled the snow-shoe goddess. Edda Snorra Sturlusonar, Gylfaginning, K. 23.

SONG OF NIÖRTHR.

I WEDDED fair Skathi,
The mountain nymph free,
And bride was there never
More winsome than she;
The crimson that dyeth
Her cheek and her lip,
Is richer than sunset
On ocean asleep—
Yet my stay was not long—
Nine nights and no more—though my love was so strong!

As lustrous and wavy
Her ringlets of gold
As cloudlets of summer,
Fold rolling o'er fold.

The voice of her laughter
Is sweet as the brook's
When he hides in the valley
'Neath moss-covered rocks.
Yet my stay was not long—
Nine nights and no more—though my love was so strong!

The towers of her father
Black crags overhung,
And downward, till evening,
Their cold shadows flung;
The sun they close followed,
Still holding, the while,
Their ice-covered mantles
'Twixt us and his smile.
So my stay was not long—
Nine nights and no more—though my love was so strong!

For how could I slumber!
All night the storm's breath

Wailed low through the valley
Like moanings of death,
Then smote, in its fury,
The fir-tree that bowed,
And snapped like a bow-string,—
The wolves howled aloud.
So my stay was not long—
Nine nights and no more—though my love was so strong!

Clouds burst on the summit,
And down its washed side
The avalanche thundered,
The hollows replied.
Then prayed I fair Skathi
To fly, the tenth morn,
With me to the sea-shore
Whereon I was born!
Thus my stay was not long—
Nine nights and no more—though my love was so strong!

SONG OF SKATHI.

Oh, Niörthr, my bridegroom,
Was comely and brave
As e'er for her lover
A maiden could crave!
But he ill brooked the mountains,
And on the tenth day,
We sought the wild sea-shore
Whereon his home lay.
Yet my stay was not long—
Nine nights and no more—though my love was so strong!

The halls of his father
Stand close by the wave;
Around the tide lashes,
The ocean gales rave.
There how could I slumber!
All night the salt foam

Dashed full at my casement—
I wept for my home—
And my stay was not long—
Nine nights and no more—though my love was so strong!

At dawn scarce I slumbered
When lo, the wild mew
Came over the water
And waked me anew!
I love not his shrieking,
I love not the roar
Of billows high breaking
Against the steep shore!
So my stay was not long—
Nine nights and no more—though my love was so strong!

Above the mad breakers,
Hoarse roaring so nigh,
I heard the poor sailor's
Last choking death cry.

At dawn, the tenth morning,
I fled to the fell,
And Niörthr fast followed,
He loved me so well;
Yet his stay was not long—
Nine nights and no more—though his love was so strong!

Again he was restless—
Grew haggard—once more
I bound on my snow-shoes,
We flew to the shore!
There soon my pale bridegroom
Refreshed him with sleep,
But I—I heard ever
The dirge of the deep!
So my stay was not long—
Nine nights and no more—though my love was so strong!

A FABLE.

A widow, poor and old and lonely,
Whose flock once numbered many a score,
Had now remaining to her only
One little lamb, and nothing more.

And every morning, forced to send it
To scanty pastures far away,
With prayers and tears did she commend it
To the good saint who named the day.

Nor so in vain; each kindly patron—
George, Agnes, Nicholas, Genevieve—
Still mindful of the helpless matron,
Brought home her lambkin safe at eve.

All-saints'-day dawns. With faith yet stronger,
On the whole hallowed choir the dame
Doth call—to one she prays no longer—
That day the wolf devoured the lamb!

THE MAID OF THE MERRY HEART.

At the sunrise hour who seeks the bower
    Of the Maid of the Merry Heart?
'Tis a soldier dight in armor bright,
    And he comes to say—"We part."

With a pleading look her hand he took,
    And his pale lips trembled long,
Ere the timid word was faintly heard—
    "One kiss—it will make me strong."

But with blushes dyed, the maid replied,
    "'Tis the victor's meed I trow!
When the laurels twine that brow of thine,
    Then the boon will I bestow."

"And if with the dead," the soldier said,
  "On the battle-field I lie,
Forever I miss the costly kiss
  That thou coldly dost deny!"

Then a playful smile she tried, the while,
  And a careless speech to frame—
"I will kiss the rose that freshly blows
  O'er thy mound of deathless fame—

"I will kiss the moss—the holy Cross
  Where it shines above thy rest—"
Ere the light words passed her tears fell fast,
  And she sunk upon his breast.

A LAY OF THE DANUBE.

I.

THE WISSEHRAD.

Pilgrim of the imperial Danube! pause 'neath yonder height,
Where a crumbling castle standeth draped in sunset light,
Like a hoary king, stout-hearted, who his throne doth fill,
Though with age he tremble, totter, clad in shining purple still!

Climb those towers, and mark the river rolling calm and wide,
Till the frowning mountain-giants dare defy his tide!
Mark where he, through flinty columns, cuts a pathway free,—
Dashes rightward, leftward, forward, throbbing, panting, toward the sea!

On those banks the angry nations gathered them of old,
Northern hordes and Southern legions joined their battles bold,
Till the dark, cold waves were flowing red and warm with blood—
Hideous Hun and haughty Roman, how they choked the crimson flood!

There, the sweet old rhymers tell us, Etzel held his court,
When he made, at Kriemhild's suing, feast for high disport,
Bidding fair her royal brothers from the distant Rhine—
Ah! ill-fated Nibelungen, wherefore did ye not divine

That an injured, vengeful woman,—though her message fell
Loving as became a sister—could not mean you well!
All in vain the pitying mermaids warned them hence to fly—
There, betrayed, the homelorn heroes died as heroes still should die!

'Neath the very towers thou scalest, now the spoil of fate,
Once a noble Magyar monarch kept his kingly state—
Great Corvinus, who Mohammed's flooding hosts could stem,
He by Rome's throned bishop counted worthiest Stephen's diadem.

There below, within the valley, lay his gallant men,
Resting from their hard-earned triumphs o'er the Saracen;
And a strange, wild tale is told us from that gray old time,
Ever still of love and sorrow—would'st thou learn it, hear my rhyme!

II.

THE MAGYAR MAID.

'Twas a day when Autumn hazes floated soft and still,
Lighter than Titania's vesture, over sky and hill;
And the sun, flushed as a lover, left the earth so fair
With his golden smiles of promise filling all the rosy air.

On the further bank a maiden stood, at that sweet hour,
Pouring o'er the bleaching linen fast the needful shower.
Humbly born this duty proved her, yet if queen might wear
On her brow such regal beauty, crown were never wanting
  there.

Now upon the turf she resteth, by the night-wind fanned,
Holding still the dripping pitcher with a careless hand,—
More like some immortal keeper of a fountain head,
Such as antique sculptures show us, than a simple mortal
  maid.

Yet the fires of shifting passion burn in her dark eye,
And her lip now smiles, now trembles, all too humanly;
Toward the camp her face still turneth through that change-
  ful cheer,
And the anxious glance she sendeth now is longing, now is
  fear.

So she leaned till twilight faded and the moon's broad beam,
Slanting o'er the hills, with silver bridged the quivering stream;
Yet she leaned, all breathless watching, till a shadow ran,
Swifter than the winged arrow, full across that shining span.

Sudden o'er those marble features shot a passing glow,
Faint as Borealis-flashes cast on Northern snow,
Then a cold and stiffening tremor shook the lovely form,
And her head fell like the lily 'neath the chariot of the storm.

Noiseless as the downy-breasted swan might touch the bank,
Came a lightly burthened shallop 'gainst the rushes dank;
To her feet the maiden started as a soldier sprung
From the bark, in warrior mantle, and his arms about her flung.

One bright smile of love all trusting on her lips there lay
Like a sunbeam, then grew colder till it died away,

And a cloud of doubt spread slowly o'er her forehead wide,
While beneath, from lids uplifted, shot the lightning-flash of
	pride.

Night's thin curtain from the lover could not hide such
	change;
Low he questioned, "My beloved, wherefore art thou
	strange?
Hath false friend or envious rival whispered cause of fear?
By Saint Stephen! but the traitor shall aby his rashness dear!"

Silent, and as one who gathers strength for utmost need,
For a moment stood the maiden, till her drooping head
Rested meek upon his shoulder—then, with rapid gest,
Back she threw the shrouding mantle—and the monarch
	stood confessed!

Swift as ever slid the wild bird from the fowler's hand,
Through his clasping arms she glided, darted toward the
	strand,

And, ere he, abashed, bewildered, of her thought was ware,
Deep beneath the rolling river plunged her shame and her despair!

Headlong the remorseful lover follows down the wave,
Catches at the floating raiment, but he cannot save—
For the hero, conscience-stricken, weakens to a child,—
On the bank once more he standeth, pale and anguish-wild!

Well, O-king, thy heart might fail thee! never from that night,
Cold and mute a spectral-shadow ceased to haunt thy sight!
Blood of Paynim, tears repentant—all in vain they flowed,
Still the sad, reproachful vision, unappeased, before thee stood.

Even yet, the reapers tell us, may that maid be seen
When the tender autumn cometh, rolling mists between;
From the parting flood she rises ere the stars are bright,
And her phantom-web outstretches far, to bleach beneath their light.

Then a tall and helmed soldier draweth to her side,
And the trembling shade doth speed her 'neath the wave to
 hide!
When the lingering years, they tell us, to a thousand run,
Only shall the lovers rest them from the long, long penance
 done.

DANIEL, THE CISTERCIAN.

In the gallery of the monastery of Osseg, one of the oldest religious foundations in Bohemia, is a picture representing a Cistercian named Daniel, whose cell is illuminated during his hours of nightly study, by a light proceeding from his own hand.

Apart, on bleak Bohemian height,
The gray old monastery stood,
Encircled by a frowning wood,
And 'twas the dead of night.

The meek Cistercian in his cell
Lay watching through that hour of gloom;
And black as vaulted, lampless tomb,
The darkness round him fell.

What shakes him? not the storm abroad—
That moves in his calm soul no fears—
But, through its awful roar, he hears ·
The still small voice of God!

" Rise! son of man, while yet 'tis night!"—
Such were the words the whisper spake—
" Rise straightway! pen and parchment take,
And what I bid thee, write!"

Even through that saintly heart there sweeps
A questioning thought, " O how obey?
Thick is the darkness, and the day
Far down the orient sleeps!"

" Rise! and thy God shall give thee light!"
Again the voice commanding said;
Abashed, he started from his bed,
And sought wherewith to write.

Scarce had his trembling fingers raised
The tablets, felt for long in vain,
When lo! the hand that touched the pen
With sudden brightness blazed!

The glory filled the narrow cell,
And, ever as the monk would write,
Still from his hand the heavenly light
Full on the parchment fell!

And *thou*—hath darkness quenched thy day?
Is Fortune's tempest wild without?
Within, the dreadful night of doubt?
In what thou *canst*, obey!

"Rise! walk!" he saith; what though thy track
A horror of great darkness hides!
First *rise*, obedient, as he bids,
And light thou shalt not lack!

THE FOUNTAIN OF THE POOR.

AN ARAB LEGEND.

Bismillah! the Merciful! Full of Compassion!
All praise be to Allah, the Lord of Creation!

Sidi Aómar—on whom be peace!—
Was the servant of God, the most high;
He was poor, yet he prayed not his goods might increase,
And his heart ever hated the lie.

Rising at dawn, in his tent's low door
With a hand ever open he stood,
Never turning his face from the old, or the poor,
Or the stranger invited of God.

Eblis, the angel that fell, was wroth
With this man of a life without blame,
And he sought before Allah, with impious mouth,
Both his faith and his works to defame.

"Sidi Aómar, thy slave," he cried,
"Is a hypocrite full of disguise!
He is poor, and because he hath naught, in his pride
Thus he feigneth him wealth to despise!

"Give him but riches till riches abound,
And his heart will soon wander from thee!
The fair slave, the fleet steed, and the flying hound
He will seek, and do service to me!"

God, the Companionless, answering, said,
"Thou art Eblis, the father of sin!
Now thy witness of falsehood be on thine own head
That the soul of my servant would'st win!"

"Give me then leave, that eftsoons I show
This Aómar as weak as the rest!"
"On the morrow, 'twixt dawn and the sunrising, go,
Put the strength of my saint to the test!

"Yet ware thee well, for, a trembling slave,
Thou shalt serve him henceforth, if thou fail!"
"Be it so," said the fiend, "and no better I crave,
If I know not the man I assail."

"Prayer," said Aómar, "is better than sleep!"
As he rose ere his eye, by the light
That so doubtfully hovered afar on the steep,
Could discern the black thread from the white.*

Solemn and glad, to the scanty well
Of his tribe, like a prophet he goes—
Lo! the pitcher, that there he hath bowed him to fill,
With the purest of silver o'erflows!

---

* The morning prayer of the faithful Mohammedan should commence as soon as he can distinguish a white thread from a black one.

"Giver of life!" said Aómar, "I sought
Not this silver, but water alone
For ablution, that pure, as the prophet hath taught,
I might send up my prayers to thy throne!"

Casting the treasure among the sands,
Yet again the full crock doth he raise—
It is brimmed, not with water for worshipping hands,
But with gold of the ruddiest blaze!

"Hearer of prayer!" said this mortal meek,
As he poured the red gold on the earth,
"Not the wealth of this world, but pure water I seek,
That for Thee hath a holier worth!"

Yet once again from the well he drew,
And behold! with a flash like the sun
At his rising, rich jewels, in gush ever new,
His rude pitcher of clay overrun.

Silent he gazed, and with troubled eye,
On the jets as they blindingly played;
Then to earth cast the crock with a penitent sigh,
And with forehead uplifted he said,

"How have I sinned, O thou Giver of good!
That this day thou dost water deny?
Must I wash then with sand like the pilgrim on road,
When he prays where no well-spring is nigh?"

Scarce had he spoke when a crystal tide
Bathed his brow with its fresh'ning spray!
And the flow of that fountain shall never be dried!
'Tis the 'Well of the Poor' to this day!

Amen! be the life of the living contrition!
The bed of the dying, the bed of submission!

THE WATER OF EL ARBAÏN.

O'er wide Arabian deserts toiling slow,
    With heat and travel spent,
With fever parched, our zemzemieh * low,
    Day after day we went.

Till now at Sinai's granite foot we lay,
    The noontide sun beat sore;
Then we arose and took our weary way
    Through sand and flints once more.

Close was the rugged valley, dry and bare,
    Walled in with adamant,
Whose sides reverberant, with blinding glare,
    Hurled back each sun-dart slant.

* Name given to the leathern water-bottle used in the East.

Yet onward still with trembling limbs we trod,
    As erst the chosen flock;
And saw where legend saith their prophet's rod
    Had cleft the eternal rock.

But thence, alas! no crystal streams now rolled
    The thirsty soul to bless;
Alone remained, of all those marvels old,
    The fiery wilderness.

At length with blackened lip and bloodshot eye,
    Scorched by the Simoom's breath,
I turned in anguish toward the brazen sky,
    And prayed for drink—or death.

Then darkness gathered o'er my swimming sight,
    Fast whirled the dizzy brain,
And the hot fever-throb, with fuller might,
    Coursed through each bursting vein.

Still to the fainting pilgrim words of cheer
    The sons of Ishmael spake,
Told of a well of living water near,
    That deathly thirst to slake;

And pointed to a verdant garden-close
    Within the vision's scope,
Where El Arbaïn's rude, shattered arches rose
    On Horeb's blasted slope.

There, pillowed soon beneath that welcome shade,
    I heard the fountain's drip,
Then felt the o'erflowing cup of coolness laid
    Against my burning lip.

Oh! never juice, drawn from the choicest vine
    Whose favored root is fed
At the pure sources of the boasted Rhine,
    Or oldest river's head,—

Nay, not Valhalla's honey'd cup so rare,
   By souls of heroes quaffed,
Not old Olympian nectar might compare
   With that divinest draught!

Cold as the ice-born flood from Northern steep,
   Clearer than Indian wave,
Sweet as nepenthe drowning care in sleep,
   A second life it gave.

O quickening fount! may thy bright currents roll
   In everlasting flow,
And on the latest wanderer's fainting soul
   A blessing like bestow!

Know, too, O mortal, thou whose rougher path
   Lies through a world of sin,
Without, the deadly arrows of its wrath,
   Its fever-fire within,—

When sorrow, doubt, despair assail thy life,
   Till thy crushed heart confess
It fain would choose, before such bitter strife,
   The grave of Nothingness,—

A well-spring, whose high source is heaven, doth wait
   Upon thy travail sore ;
There drink! and thou shalt rise as re-create,
   Nor thirst for evermore !

AXEL.

FROM THE SWEDISH OF TEGNÉR.

Esaias Tegnér, Bishop of Wexiö, the greatest of Swedish poets, was born in 1782, and after a distinguished academical as well as professional career, died in 1846. His most celebrated work is *Frithiof's Saga*, which has been made accessible to the English-speaking public by five or six translations, none of them, however, by any means satisfactory. But his reputation was first established by several lyrical pieces, by the *Children of the Supper*, so finely rendered by Longfellow, and by Axel, a version of which is here given in the metre of the original. When the present translation was made, the author of it was not aware that Axel had ever appeared in an English dress, but she has recently seen parts of a version by Latham, and a complete one by Bethune. The former of these would not have deterred her from undertaking another, and she hopes that the one here offered may not be found inferior even to the latter in closeness of conformity to the spirit and letter of the original.

> The olden time is dear to me,
> The olden time of Charles's glory,
> Gladsome as conscience pure, its story,
> And spirited as victory.
> In Northern lands, its reflex even

Yet lingers on the verge of heaven,
And forms majestic come and go,
In yellow belt and tunic blue,
Where red the sky of evening burneth.
With awe mine eye upon you turneth,
Ye heroes of an age more bright,
With martial buff and broad-sword dight!

One veteran from that age victorious,—
In childhood's days I knew him well—
Erect he stood amongst us still,
A trophy ruined, but yet glorious.
With silver of a century shone
His locks, (to him none else was given,)
And on his brow deep scars were graven
Like runes on monumental stone.
True he was poor; yet he but jested
With poverty, familiar grown;
Frugal as in the field, alone
Within his woodland hut he rested.

Two treasures did the old man own,
'Gainst which earth's wealth as nothing weighed,
His Bible, and his trusty blade
With CHARLES THE TWELFTH writ fair thereon.
The great king's deeds, now found recited,
Where countless pens have them indited,
(For wide that eagle flew around,)
Stood in his memory recorded,
Ranged like the urns of warriors hoarded
Within a grassy funeral mound.
When he some great exploit was showing
Of young King Charles, his 'blue boys' bold,
How high he held his forehead old,
With what a fire his eye was glowing!
And from his lips each word that fell
Rung like the clash of smiting steel.
Far into night he often sat
Talking of former days so famed,
And never, when King Charles was named,
Would fail to lift his well-worn hat,

Wondering I stood beside his knee,
(For scarcely higher reached my head,)
And pictures of those heroes dead
From boyhood still remain to me,
And tales now half-forgotten lie
Dimly within my memory,
As 'neath the snow sleeps in its seed
The lily, when its flower is fled.

Peace to his ashes! they repose
Long since within the quiet earth.
The saga his; take it, O North,
And weep with me o'er AXEL's woes!
But 'gainst the old man's words of flame
My simple rhymes must needs be tame.

The mighty monarch lay at Bender;
His wasted lands had no defender,
Disgraced his name, so glorious late,
And as a wounded champion yet

Fights, though on bended knee, and feeling
The chill of death upon him stealing,
So fought each man behind his shield,
Desperate, but scorning still to yield;
For hope of rescue there was none
In any breast save his alone.
The king, though hurricanes were shaking
The leaves of fate, though earth seemed quaking,
Stood calm as arch that hath defied
The bursting bomb 'mid ruins wide,
Or rock that breasts the raging wave,
Or Fortitude beside a grave.

One evening he to AXEL said,
"Take thou this letter!"—and he laid
The missive in his hand—" now ride
Towards Sweden straight, this even-tide.
See that thou rest not, day or night,
Till our old mountains greet thy sight;

Before my council there thou'lt lay
The letter—and God speed thy way!"

Young Axel loves to ride amain!
The letter in his belt with joy
He hides.   His sire, at Holofzin,
Fell fighting by his king; the boy—
Thenceforth the camp's adopted child—
Grew up 'mid wars and tumults wild.
'Twas a fair form, such as our North
Doth sometimes even yet bring forth,
Fresh as a rose, but tall and slim
As Sweden's firs in youthful prime.
His archèd brow was high and clear
As heaven's vault when no cloud is there,
And every feature bore impress
Of frankness and of earnestness.
His eye transparent seemed as given
To look with hope and confidence
Up to the God of day in Heaven,

Yet without fear to turn their glance
Downward to him, who, shorn of light,
Dwells 'neath the shadow of the night.—

In the king's guard 'twas his to hold
A place among his soul's own kin;
A little band, whose number told
Seven, like the stars of Charles's Wain,
Or, like the Muses, nine at most,
All strictly chosen from the host;
By fire and sword proved well and long,
A troop of Christian vikings strong,
Not unlike those who whilom clave
With dragon-ships the dark-blue wave.
Within no bed might they repose;
On the hard earth their cloaks they spread,
And there, mid storms and drifting snows,
Slept calmly as on flowery mead.
A horse-shoe with the naked hand
They twisted. None e'er saw them stand

Round chimney fires; they rather chose
The warmth of heated ball that glows
Red as the day-star, when he sets
In blood on Northern winter nights.
It was their law, that on the field
To less than seven one might not yield,
E'en in retreat must face the foe,
A flying back they might not show.
Lastly, this law—and harder yet,
Perhaps, than all the rest beside—
None on a maid his heart might set,
Till Charles himself should take a bride.
Though eyes of heavenly blue might shine,
Or rosy lips wear smiles divine,
However snowy breasts might heave,
Like swans rocked on the limpid wave,
Nor eye nor heart the charm must feel,
For each was married to his steel.

Young Axel saddled glad his steed,

And rode both day and night with speed,
Till he on Ukraine's border stood—
A flash of steel within the wood!
Sabres and lances quick upspring,
And round him close a glittering ring.
" Dispatches thou dost bear from Bender;
Dismount, and to my hand surrender
Thy charge,—or die!" His ready blade
A plain, a Swedish answer made;
Grown sudden meek, the speaker bowed
To earth, and weltered in his blood.
With back against an oak-tree stayed,
His desperate game the hero played.
At every whiz of his good sword
A knee was bowed, and life-blood poured.
Nobly he kept the oath they made—
One against seven—why, that were naught!
One against twenty, flew his blade.
He fought as once Rolf Krake fought,
Striving, since hope of life was none,

For company in death alone;
And gashes purple-lipped declare
His fate inevitably near;
The blood around his heart grows chill,
His hand, though glued to sword-hilt still,
Is numbed; thick shadows veil his sight,
And faint he sinks to darkest night.

Halloo! the woods are echoing round!
And falcon bold, and trusty hound
Pursue their game. Behold! a troop
Of flying huntsmen gallops up,
And, dashing foremost of the train,
On dappled steed, in habit green,
With rosy cheeks, fair as the sun,
Rides, whirlwind like, an amazon.
The robber-band affrighted fled,
Her courser started at the dead;
Then with a bound she leaped to earth—
And there he lay, stretched like an oak

Among the brushwood, by the stroke
Of a fierce tempest from the north.
How fair he seemed, though bathed in blood!
And leaning over him now stood,
MARIA, as once Dian fair
Descending from her heavenly sphere,
On Latmos, from the chase withdrawn,
Stood over her Endymion.
The sleeper that enchanted her
Than this could not be lovelier.
Within his pierced and mangled breast
A spark of life yet feebly glows,
And straight her followers frame in haste
A litter of the greenwood boughs;
And placing him thereon with care,
They bear him to her dwelling near.

The maiden sat beside his bed,
 With pity filled and anxious dread,
And on those features pale she cast

A look whose worth a realm surpassed;
She sat beside him like a rose,
In fair but now fast wasting Greece,
Wild and luxuriant that grows
Beside a fallen Hercules.
At length from deathly swoon he wakes,
Looks round amazed, and hurried speaks.
Alas! his eyes, but late so mild,
Have suddenly grown fixed and wild.
" Where am I?   Girl, what wouldst thou have?
No woman's eye may rest on me,
No tears of thine my wounds may lave!
To Charles I've sworn it solemnly.
My father walks the Milky Way!
He's wroth! that oath he heard me say!
And yet how fair to mortal sense
The enchantress!   Demon! get thee hence!
Where is my belt?   My letter and—
'Twas written by the king's own hand!
My father's sword is good!   It bites

Right greedily the Muscovites
What joy to strike, and see them fall!
Oh, that King Charles had witnessed all!
They fell like grain before the knife!
I half seemed wounded in the strife.—
The letter I to Stockholm bear,
My honor's pledged to take it there.
Dear are the moments! Up! to horse!"—
Such, wild with fever, his discourse;
And then the hero deathly pale
Back on his quiet pillow fell.

Then death contended long with life
Over the youth in doubtful strife.
Life conquered; slow the peril passed.
And Axel now could view, at last,
With conscious eye, though weak and dim,
The angel that still watched by him,—
Not one of those idyllic maids,
Who sighing walk in verdant shades,

A counterfeit of pining thought,
With tresses yellow as the light,
Cheeks pale as violet of the night,
And eyes like the forget-me-not.
Eastern her blood; her black locks lie,
Like midnight round a bed of roses,
Where on her forehead bold and high
Glad courage—the sole true—reposes;
Like victory graven on the shield
That warrior-maiden bears in field.
Her hue fresh as in painters' dreams
Aurora crowned with radiant beams;
In form she seemed an Oread,
And dancing was her step and glad.
And high her swelling bosom heaves
With youth and health; together weaves
The lily with the rose her frame;
Her soul a pure ethereal flame,
A southern summer-heaven complete
With sun and flowery odors sweet.

And in her eye's dark glance there strove
A heavenly and an earthly light,
Now flashing like the bird of Jove
Proudly from the empyrean height,
Now mild as Aphrodite's doves
Drawing the chariot of the Loves.

O, Axel! of thy wounds the smart
Soon passes, only scars remain;
Without, thy breast is cured of pain;
But ah! how fares it with thy heart?
Look not so loving on the hand
That binds thy wounds with healing band—
The hand that white as marble shows—
In thine it never may repose!
It bears more peril to thy peace
Than those hard hands of Osmanlis,
That late at Bender thou hast seen
With sabre armed and carabine.
Those fresh red lips, that only ope

To breathe of comfort and of hope,
In tones as from the spirit-world—
'Twere better thou shouldst hear again
On Pultowa's ensanguined plain
The thunderbolts Czar Peter hurled!
When, trembling and with pallid mien,
Thou goest to breathe the summer balm,
On thine own sword, O Axel! lean,
And not upon that rounded arm,
Which seems as 'twere by Cupid made
To be the pillow for his head.

Wonder of heaven and earth! O, Love!
Thou breath from blissful realms above!
Spark of Divinity, that cheers
Our darkness in this vale of tears!
In Nature's breast the beating heart,
Comfort of Gods and men thou art!
Drop seeketh drop in ocean's bed,
And all the stars above us tread,

Whirling from pole to pole, each one

A bridal dance around its sun.

Still art thou to the human soul

A reflex, faint memorial,

Of brighter, better days, when, even

Yet but a child, she dwelt in heaven—

That azure hall, whose roof is set

With many a starry crown of light,

Where nightly she, with joy o'erblest,

Sank in her father's arms to rest.

Rich as the gifts of fancy are,

Her only language then was prayer,

And every fair and winged child

Of heaven on her a brother smiled.

She fell to earth! since that, not even

Her love is pure; yet doth she trace,

With joy, in the beloved's face,

Some look of former friends in heaven;

And song of poet or of spring

Doth to her ear their lost tones bring.

Oh, happy is the exile then,
As wandering Swiss, who hears again
Some note of home, that doth restore
Boyhood and Alpine heights once more!

'Twas evening! Twilight wrapped in gold
Lay dreaming on her western bed,
And, mute as Egypt's priests of old,
The stars their solemn marches led.
And earth below that sky so fair
Stood like a bride, in whose dark hair
Rich gems are flashing, blush and smile
Playing beneath her veil the while.
Tired with the pleasures of the day,
In smiling sleep the Naiad lay,
And tranquil Evening sat at rest,
A red rose shining on her breast.
The little Cupids, that had lain
Bound by the sunshine, free again,
Now gaily on the moonbeams ride,

With bow and quiver at their side,

Where Spring, through greenwood arches, late

Made entry in triumphal state.

Forth from the oak the nightingale

Strikes out her song that fills the vale—

Soft, innocent, and pure that strain,

As some sweet lyric of Franzén.

In all, it seemed as Nature said,

' Behold, the hour for tryst is made ! '

All life, yet silence so complete,

Thou mightst have heard her great heart beat.—

Then, conscious of the happy charm,

The youthful pair walked arm in arm.

As plighted lovers rings, so these

Exchanged their childhood's memories.

He talked of bright days when he dwelt

'Neath the red roof maternal, built

Of the hewn fir-tree, and that rose

Among the pines mid Northern snows ;

Of the dear land where he was bred;
Brothers and sisters long since dead.
He told, as well, how, many a time,
The old, the deep heroic rhyme,
And saga-volume parchment-bound,
Had wakened longings so profound
For great exploit.   In dreams of night
He seemed a warrior armed for fight,
And mounted on the tall steed Grane,
Like mythic Sigurd Fafnisbane,
He rode through magic fire-wall straight
To sage Brynhilda's castle gate,
That flaming in the moonlight stood,
Encircled by a laurel wood.
The house grew close, his breath not free,
Then to the forest would he flee,
And climbing, with a boy's delight,
The fir-top where the eagles light,
Would sit, rocked by the northern blast,
Till cheek and heart were cooled at last.

What joy to mount the swift cloud-car
That rolls above him, and afar
Be borne beyond the narrow seas
Out to a fairer world than this,
Where Victory beckons, Glory stands,
Chaplets for heroes in her hands,
And where King Charles, (whom scarce he owns
Seven years his senior), plucketh crowns
With his good sword, and instantly—
O how divine!—gives them away!
" At fifteen, could my mother's fears
No longer keep me; bathed in tears
I fell upon her bosom; then
Toward Poland turned my steps, since when,
As watch-fire steady, my life's flame
Hath burned amid the battle-game.
Yet never parent bird I see
Feeding its young caressingly,
Never upon a fair child look
Playing with flowers beside the brook,

But, sudden, war's attractions cease,
And in my soul sweet thoughts of Peace
Arise, with groves and golden grain,
And laughing children in her train;
And by a quiet cottage door,
The rosy twilight glowing o'er
Her face, a maiden stands, the same
That oft has blessed my boyhood's dream.
Of late, these images of rest
My soul unceasing have possessed.
I close my eyelids; they appear
Only more life-like and more clear,
And she who crowneth every scene—
Maria! thou art still that queen!"

Confused and blushing said the maid,
"Happy the lot of man indeed!
Strong man! no fetter beareth he,
E'en from his childhood, is he free.
And danger's charms, and glory's crown,

And heaven and earth are all his own.
But woman—hers a different lot!
Man's mere appendage to the last;
A bandage for his wounds; forgot
Soon as the fretting pain is past!
She is the offering, he the fire
That glorious heavenward doth aspire!—
My sire in Peter's wars did fall,
My mother's face I scarce recall.
The desert's daughter grew up wild
Within these walls, an idol child
Honored by slaves, who meek endure
Each vain caprice of tyrant power.
A noble spirit feels its shame,
Dwelling with souls so basely tame!
Hast ever on our boundless plain
Seen the wild steed of noble strain?
Fiery as hero, fleet as hind,
He scorns to own a master's care;
With ears erect, turned to the wind,

He stands and scents the danger near,
Then scouring in a whirlwind cloud
Of dust, o'er the wide steppe he flies,
Fights his own fights with hoof unshod,
Untamed enjoys, untamed he dies!
'Sons of the wilderness so free,
How fair, how blest, your life must be!'
I cried, and bade them check their speed,
Whene'er my neighing Tatar steed,
A bitted slave, e'en to a word
Obedient, bore me to the herd;
But the troop heeded not my cry,
And, scornful snorting, thundered by.
Nor could my spirit free as air
The castle's endless sameness bear;
With zeal I learned the sylvan war,
'Gainst bird and beast of prey went forth,
And oft scarce saved from paw of bear
A life that only then had worth.
But ah! we bend not Nature's will;

AXEL.

In lowly hut, or on the throne,
A seamstress or an amazon,
The woman is the woman still;
A vine that droops if naught sustain,
A being of its half forlorn,
To whom all joys unshared are vain,
Whose every pleasure is twin-born!
This quick pulsation that is fraught
With suffering, yet a joy to feel—
This longing for I know not what,
So painful and so gladsome still—
It hath no aim, it hath no bound;
As if on wings, I leave the ground
And soar to Heaven, whose starry dome
Of blest immortals is the home,
Then downward to the earth I fall,
To you, dear forms! familiar all;
Ye trees that with me have grown up,
Thou hillock with thy flowery top,
Thou brook with all thy songs of love—

I've seen, I've heard you, all these years,
But as a statue sees and hears.
Now first, now first, my heart ye move!
I feel my soul, less selfish grown,
Is of a purer, higher tone
Since first,"—but here a sudden red
The maiden's features overspread;
She paused; a smothered sigh confessed
The thought her words but half expressed.

His song renews the nightingale,
While lists the moon, 'neath cloudy veil;
And in a long unending kiss
As warm as life, nor faithful less
Than the still grave, their souls, set free,
Melted in one blest harmony!
They kissed as on the altar-stone
Two flames kiss and become but one,
Which, glowing with a stronger light,
Soars loftier in its heavenward flight.

For them, gone was this world of ill,
And Time in mid career stood still.
Of this poor mortal life each hour
Is bounded, meted by time's power,
Love's kiss and death's alone may be
Named children of eternity.
The happy pair! in fire earth's frame
Might roll, they would not see the flame;
The firmament of heaven might rock
And fall, they would not hear the shock!
The Genius of the North and South,
Thus had they stood with mouth to mouth,
And passed, unconscious, in that kiss,
From earthly into heavenly bliss!

From that elysian flight, earthward
Came Axel first. "Now by my sword,
By the pure honor of the North,
And by yon stars that there stand forth
Like white-robed bridemaids shining down,

For earth and heaven thou art mine own!
Far, far removed from war, what bliss,
Within some friendly vale, where peace
Sheltered by mountains dwelleth free,
Could I but live and die with thee!
But ah! an oath my soul doth chain!
With pallid cheek and glance of ire,
It lays an icy hand between
Our hearts that burn with holy fire.
But fear not! all shall yet be well!
Redeemed, but never broken, shall
Mine oath be! Now I must away!
When to her feast of flowers fair May
Next bids us, I am here again
To fetch my bride, my wife!—till then,
Sweet maid, than life more dear to me,
Half of my soul! farewell to thee!"

He spoke,—and turning at the word,
Reclasped his belt, resumed his sword,

And straight set forth, his journey through
The Czar's wide empire to pursue.
Concealed within the woods by day,
By night he held his rapid way
Towards heaven's firm key-stone, shining forth
The changeless pole-star of our North.
And gentle Charles's Wain, that yet
In ocean s waves hatn never set,
That wain with shafts all silver bright,
And wheels that blaze with golden light.
And now, a thousand perils past,
Through hostile troops he comes at last
To Sweden's capital, that hears,
With wonder, what her hero dares,
And to the councillors the king's
Letter and greeting faithful brings.

Meanwhile, within her lonely halls
On Axel's name Maria calls;
She sighs it through the woods profound,

Teaches the hills and vales its sound.
" What oath can hold him in its band?
Some maiden of his native land?
Some former love? can this be true?
My heart protests there ne'er are two!
Thou snow-veiled maiden of the North,
Or one of us must die, or both!
The Southern fire thou dost not know!
Far as thy frozen lakes may lie
Among thy mountains clad in snow,
I'll seek thee! thou shalt surely die!
But stay!—a child he left the North,
Nor since, the country of his birth
Hath seen, and from the camp's fierce cry
Love, timid Love, is wont to fly.
No stain on brow that's arched like thine!
There only truth and honor shine.
In thy pure glance I've read the whole,
The deepest secret of thy soul,
As the keen eye of day looks through

The fount's clear depths of silvery blue.
Why fleest thou then? And doth that vow
Bind thee my heart to break? And how—
But ah! in space my murmurs die!
A widow among graves I sigh,
A dove, that heaven and earth doth fill
With her complaints unanswered still!
Ah! forests sigh and billows flow
Between us, and he hears me not.
What if I follow! But, oh no!
That for a woman ill were thought.
A woman! Who shall know? I'll wear
A sword, and lo! the man is there!
With peril have I often played,
For life and death a die-cast made;
As grown to courser, bold I ride,
My bullet ne'er hath swerved aside.
Some angel prompteth this design—
Now Axel, Axel! thou art mine!
I'll seek thee in the distant North,

I'll seek thee through the wide, wide earth,
From shore to shore, from dell to dell,
And force thee that same oath to tell!
Bear me, O War! upon thy wing,
Till me to Axel's land thou bring!"

Thus spoke the maid; so said, so done!
Resolve and action are but one
With woman. Lo! the change complete!
The helmet hides her locks of jet,
Strong buff her bosom's wealth enfolds,
Powder and ball her knapsack holds,
And o'er her shoulders white and fine,
Death's engine hangs, a carabine.
From girdle like fair Dian's zone,
Pendent a flashing sabre shone,
And round her lips she drew a shade,
Of downy beard that semblance made,
And much it seemed as one should choose
With dusky crape to wreathe a rose.

With belt and sword how like she grew
To Cupid turned a hero too,
As blazoned on the glittering shield
The son of Clinias bore in field!
"Home of my fathers, fare thee well!
I trust, in love and peace I may
Return, once more in thee to dwell;
But now I can no longer stay.
Fold me within thy veil, O Night!
And to my Axel aid my flight!"—

Already on a border won
Under the eyelid of the North
Grown drowsy, stood Czar Peter's town.
There mortgaged crowns from the whole earth
Are gathered now; then in its creek
Still small it lay, but dragon-like.
It shows the serpent, though so young;
As in the sun-warmed sand he coils,
He hisses with his forked tongue,

Within his fangs the venom boils.
'Gainst Sweden, armed with fire and sword
There lay a squadron; thitherward
Maria bent her course, and where
Swords glance and banners flout the air,
She seeks a place on board the fleet
That soon the Swedish hosts shall meet.
The leader of that savage horde
Eyed her full sharply, with the word,
"More dangerous, methinks, young swain!
Thou'lt prove to Northern maids than men.
We'll send thee! 'tis not to be feared
That they will pluck thee by the beard!
But war's stern art thou'lt learn from them
Right thoroughly. 'Tis no child's game;
For life and death the venture's tried,
God and Saint Nicholas decide!"

The sails fill fast, the keels ride free
In foam upon the Baltic sea;

Soon in the sunset's glowing light
The Swedish mountains rise to sight,
Defying time and tide they stand,
A giant beacon nature-planned.
They landed then at Sotaskär—
A name to faithful hearts most dear—
There for the last time Hjalmar parted
With Ingeborg, there broken-hearted
Died the fair maid, when ODIN's call
Summoned her hero to his hall.
Around that cliff her soul doth hover
Sorrowing e'en yet for her lost lover.
Leucadia of the North! thy fame
Once great in saga, now forgot!
But Hjalmar's death-song keeps thy name,
And poet-hearts forsake thee not!

From town to town the flames blaze high,
The children shriek, the women fly,
For Russian warfare well they know;

And all the neighboring country through,
Both night and day the church-bells swing—
But naught thy dead to life can bring,
Thou land bereaved! Thy champions bold,
Thy towers of strength, the grave doth hold!
But Sweden's danger now calls forth
Old men and boys to save their North,
With swords that served Gustavus, when
Blood on Germania's soil was spilt,
And halberds that had crossed the Belt,
Now blunt, but used to victory then;
And many a blunderbuss appears
Whose rusty matchlock proves its years.
'Twas all that Sweden still possessed—
A little troop, and, for the rest,
Ill armed, but without doubt or fear
Against the invader they draw near.
But 'twas no fight of man to man!
Round him a cloud the foeman threw,
And from the cliff courage in vain

Would seek to scale, his lightnings flew,
And, unchastised, Death's tireless hand
Mowed the thin ranks of that small band.

As comes the avenging god of war
With belt and hammer, angry THOR,
So Axel to the field, where dread
And flight are reigning, hurrieth,
A succoring angel sent in need!
His breast is steel, his arm is death,
The Swedes he rallies; left and right
He flies upon his courser white.
"Stand, friends! close up your ranks anew!
From Charles, our king, I come to you,
From his own lips a greeting bring,
Our watchword still, God and the King!"
"God and King Charles!" echoes through all
Their lines; they heed the hero's call.
The height whence pours that shower of death
Is stormed and taken in a breath,

Silenced the cannon's roar; like grain
Weapons and corpses strew the plain,
And swords smite blindly, but right true,
The necks of that wild flying crew,
And, panic-struck, the robber band,
Slipping their cables, leave the strand.

Sleeping, like glutted beast of prey,
Upon the field grim Slaughter lay.
From heaven's pavilion shone the moon
Upon that desolation down.
Along the shore by night o'erspread,
Walked Axel sighing 'mong the dead.
In couples lying, how they clasp
Each other! deathly strong that grasp!
A true embrace would'st thou behold,
Look not on lovers, who enfold
Each other smiling; go
Forth rather to the battle! see
How to his heart foe presseth foe,

AXEL.

In the last dying agony!
"Transports of love and pleasure pass
Swiftly as doth spring's fleeting breath;
But hate and pain and woe, alas!
Are faithful even unto death."
Thus sighing, sudden doth he shrink
To hear a voice complaining cry,
"I thirst, O Axel! give me drink!
Receive my farewell ere I die!"
Those tones familiar! at the sound,
He clears the steep height with a bound.
Lo! leaning 'gainst the rock, there stood
A stranger, wounded, bathed in blood.
Forth from a cloud the moon's bright glance
Fell on that pallid countenance;
With a wild shriek of horror, he
Cries shudderingly, "O God! 'tis she!"
'Twas she indeed! Her wounds' deep smart
Hiding, her whisper faintly fell;
"Oh, welcome, Axel!—No, farewell!

Death's chills are gathering round my heart!
Oh! ask not what hath brought me here!
'Tis love alone hath made me err!
When shades of endless night come o'er us,
And the tomb's gate stands close before us,
How different then this life appears!
How small its sorrows and its cares!
Love only, blameless, pure like ours,
Goes with us to the heavenly bowers.
Thine oath, that I have sought to know,
To me the shining stars will show;
There it stands written; I shall see,
As clear as they, thy truth to me.—
I know I have done thoughtlessly,
I know thou sorrowest sore for me!
Forgive me—for love's sake thou must!—
Each tear thou sheddest o'er my dust.
Parent or brother I had none,
But thou to me wert all in one;
Thou wert my all!—O Axel swear,

That even in death thou hold'st me dear!—
Thou swearest!—Wherefore murmur I?
For life, of all her poesy
The fairest, best, hath dealt to me;
Thy bride!—and on thy heart to die!
And shall not now my dust repose
On soil thou'st saved from its foes?
Axel, behold! over the moon
A cloud is passing; when 'tis flown,
Then I depart; my soul shall stand
Transfigured on the heavenly land
Praying for thee, and from the skies
Watch o'er thee with immortal eyes.
Plant by my grave a southern rose,
And when it dies 'neath winter snows—
Child of the sun—think of thy bride,
Who lieth sleeping by its side.
Brief was her bloom!—But, Axel, see!
The cloud is gone, my spirit free!

Farewell, farewell!" faintly she sighs,
Convulsive grasps his hand—and dies.

Forth from the Stygian flood, not Death,
But his young brother, MADNESS, rose.
His face is pale, a poppy wreath
Amid his locks dishevelled shows;
By turns he gazes on the ground,
By turns looks upward to the skies;
His mouth convulsed a smile plays round,
And tears bedim his half-shut eyes.
Poor Axel's head with wand of power
He touched, and ever from that hour
The youth with ceaseless step doth walk
Around the grave, as sagas say
In olden time the dead would stalk
Round where their buried treasures lay.
And day and night that shore so lone
Echoes his sad and touching moan.

AXEL.

"Hush, hush! thou blue and billowy sea,
Against the shore, oh, beat not so!
For in my dreams thou troublest me;
I do not love to hear thy flow.
Thy foaming waves with blood are red;
And Death upon my shore thou'st led.
But late, a youth here bleeding lay,
I made his grave with roses gay;
For he was like——I well know whom!
I'll bring her home, when spring doth bloom.
They tell me that my bride doth rest
In earth,—that o'er her faithful breast
The green sod grows;—Oh, no! herself
Last night upon that rocky shelf
I saw, pale as they paint the dead,
But that was from the moonbeam's light.—
O'er lip and cheek a chillness spread,
'Twas from the cold wind of the night.—
I prayed the lovely shape to stay;
She laid her finger on my brow

So dark and heavy; then it grew
As light and joyous as the day.
How shone they in the far, far East,
Those days departed! Oh, how blest
Were they, how heavenly and how fair!
How happy was poor Axel there!
A castle stood deep in a grove,
It was the mansion of my love.
Pierced, dying, in a wood apart
I lay, life gave she with a kiss,
To my embrace she gave her heart,
That heart so warm, so rich in bliss!
Now in her faded breast, like stone
It lieth cold!—and all is gone!
Ye stars that burn in yonder sky,
I pray you, quench your light and die!
I knew a morning-star so bright—
A sea of blood hath drowned its light!
The scent of blood breathes from the strand,
Its crimson stain is on my hand!"—

Such was the wail on Sotaskär!
When the day kindled, he was there,
Nor turned away at fall of eve,
But lingered still to watch and grieve.
Dead on that shore one morn he sat,
With folded hands, as if in prayer,
On the pale cheek tears resting, that
Were stiffened by the frosty air,
And on the grave wherein she slept
His eyes, though glazed in death, he kept.

Such was the saga that I heard.
How deep, how tenderly it stirred!
Full thirty winters since have strewn
Their snows; my heart preserves it still;
For childhood's fancies sharply drawn,
With outline clear, are graven well
Upon the poet's soul; there they,—
As in King Heimer's harp once lay

Fair Aslög *—rest, till starting forth,
Like her they prove their noble birth
With gorgeous robes and bearing high,
And golden hair and kingly eye.
Oh! childhood's heaven doth ever hold
Its countles lyres of ruddy gold;
Whate'er the bard doth later sing,
Heroic deeds, or flowers of spring,
In fairer forms all hath passed by,
In earlier days, his childhood's eye.
Still, when in verdant spring the quail
Strikes out his music in the vale,
And Luna from the eastern wave
Starts like a spectre from the grave,

---

* Aslög or Aslaug was the daughter of Sigurd Fafnisbani, (slayer of the dragon Fafnir,) a sort of Scandinavian Hercules, and Brynhilda. At the death of her father and mother she was three years old, and Heimir, Brynhilda's foster-father, fearing for her the hostility of family enemies, concealed her, with splendid garments and much treasure, in a large harp, with which he wandered about as a mendicant musician. The rich clothing having been observed through an opening in the harp, by the mistress of the cottage where they lodged, she incited her husband to kill Heimir, and the harp being broken open, Aslög was discovered. Sigurd is a favorite hero of the Scandinavian mythic legends, and his life and exploits form the principal subject of the Icelandic Völsunga-Saga.

And painteth hill and painteth dale
So sadly with death's color pale,
Then sighs this ballad in mine ear,
And yet again I seem to hear
The song learned at the old man's side,
Of Axel and his Russian bride.

SONG OF THE LAPLAND LOVER.

FROM THE SWEDISH OF FRANZEN.

Francis Michael Franzén was born at Uleåborg in Finland, in 1772, but retired to Sweden, when that province was ceded to Russia, and became Bishop of Hörnöesand, in which position he remained until his death in 1847. He was among the most conspicuous and active members of the Swedish Academy, and his poems, the best of which are of a simple, natural, idyllic character, are deservedly popular in Sweden. The following song has been especially admired.

Spring, my reindeer swift!

Over field and fell!

Where my girl doth dwell

Thou shalt paw the drift!

There the mosses grow

Thick beneath the snow!

Ah, how short the day!

And the way so long!

Spring, then, at my song!
Let us haste away!
Rest thou may'st not here!
Wolves are ever near!

See, there flies the ern!
Blest the winged indeed!
See yon cloudlet speed!
Were I on it borne,
I had now erewhile
Seen thy far-off smile.

Thou, this heart that hast
Quickly made thy prey—
Thus the wild deer they
To the tame make fast—
Cataract-strong to thee
Down thou drawest me!

Since thy face I've known,
Thoughts by thousands flit

Through me, day and night—
Thousands, yet but one!
All in one combine—
How to make thee mine!

Thou, to hide, may'st lie
'Mong the rocks below —
Where the fir-woods grow,
With thy reindeer fly—
Away, away, for me
Shall both rock and tree!

Spring, my reindeer swift!
Over field and fell!
Where my girl doth dwell
Thou shalt paw the drift!
There the mosses grow
Thick beneath the snow!

THE MOSS-ROSE.

FROM THE GERMAN OF HELMINE VON CHEZY, GEB. VON KLENKE.

Deep in a dell, 'neath woodland shade,
The green and tender moss was spread,
    A carpet velvet-soft.
Small to the eye indeed, yet still
Its tree-like form was wonderful—
    Branch, bough and leafy tuft.

The low moss saw the wood's green pride,
The blushing rose; "Such pomp," it sighed,
    "Heaven hath refused me quite.
Here many a light foot treadeth free,
But not an eye doth look on me—
    All turn them to the light!"

Lo! through that grove, when twilight glows,
With wandering step the Saviour goes,
    His features pale and wan;
'Twas grateful when the soft moss met
So closely round His bleeding feet
    That still must journey on.

Late had he left the desert land
Where fiercely burned the sun and sand—
    The soft moss cooled His heat;
Then spake the Saviour, "From above
On thee hath been bestowed such love,
    So earnest, tender, great!

"In the slight form assigned to thee
Was ever eye too blind to see
    The Maker's power and grace?
Thou little plant so lightly prized,
Thee hath thy Father not despised,
    Be patient in thy place!"

Scarce had the Saviour spoken thus,
When, suddenly, springs from the moss
    A rose most fair to see.
From it the name of moss-rose comes,
And now in every land it blooms,
    Sweet type of modesty.

Into Christ's earthly cup some sweet
The moss had poured—had kissed His feet;
    This its reward at last.
O heart, still true and tender rest,
If, like the moss, thou art depressed,
    The rose is budding fast!

THE GLOW-WORM.

FROM THE GERMAN OF HELMINE VON CHEZY, GEB. VON KLENKE.

The blessed John once walked beside
A limpid stream, and watched its tide.
Through grass and flowers his pathway lies,
He marks them well with loving eyes,
So fresh their bloom, so fair to sight—
' Oh, God, this earth of Thine how bright !
The little floweret smiling still
While buds and verdure fill the vale !
There's not a leaf or flower, I ween,
But hath a sense of life within.
Each little worm, though meanly dressed,
Is in its conscious being blessed.
Where'er a spark of life doth dwell
The love of God abideth still !'

With glowing heart thus musing, he
Upon the earth a worm doth see;
A poor, gray thing, of make so slight
His foot had well-nigh crushed it quite.
He lifted it, with tender care,
And placed it on a blossom fair.
"Live, live!" the loved disciple said,
"For thee, too, were spring's bounties shed!"
The touch scarce felt that little frame,
When a quick sense of blessing came;
Love's warmth through every fibre flows,
And lo, with pleasing light it glows!
Wings grow apace, and him they bear
Through the wide pathway of the air;
O'er tree tops, on soft gales of night,
He floats as flashing emerald bright,
Or, spread upon a flower, he lies
Like a star fallen from the skies;
Soft on the turf then sinks that ray,
And, loving still, doth pale away.

A GODLIE HYMNE,

INDITED BY HULDRYCH ZWINGLE, WHEN HE WAS SMITTEN OF YE PESTILENCE.

I. *In ye begynninge of hys maladye.*

Lorde God, helpe mee
In this my neede!
I thinke indeede
Dethe's at the doore.

EIN CHRISTENLICH GSANG,

GESTELLT DURCH HULDRYCH ZWINGLI, ALS ER MIT PESTILENZ ANGGRIFFEN WARD.

I. *Im Anfang der Krankheit.*

Hilf, herr gott, hilf
In diser not!
Ich mein der tod
Syg an der thür.

A GODLIE HYMNE.

Stonde Thou before

Mee, Christ, for Thou hast vanquisht Dethe!

I crye to Thee;

Plucke, if Thou wille,

The shafte oute stille,

That woundeth sore,

And not an houre

Dothe let me drawe in peace my brethe!

If Thou decree

That I shal be

Dethe's praye, my dayes halfe ronne,

Stand, Christe, für,
Dann du in überwunden hast.
Zuo dir ich gilf:
Ist es din will,
Züch us den pfyl
Der mich verwundt;
Nit lass ein stund
Mich haben weder ruow noch rast.
Willt du dann glych
Tod haben mich
Inmitts der tagen min,

So thenne, Thy wille be done!

Doe Thou Thy choyce;

I have no voyce;

Thy creature stille

Make whole, or spille!

And callest Thou

My spirit nowe

Awaye from tyme,

Thou sav'st it from alle worser cryme,

And ne'er againe·

Another's soule 'twill tainct wyth sinne.

So soll es willig syn.
Thuo wie du willt:
Mich nüt befilt.
Din haf bin ich:
Mach ganz ald brich.
Dann nimmst du hin
Den geiste min
Von diser erd,
Thuost dus dass er nit bœser werd
Ald andern nit
Befleck ir leben fromm und sitt.

A GODLIE HYMNE.

II. *In the middest of ye disease.*

Give comfort, Lorde!

Mine ill doth waxe,

My frame paine rackes,

My spirit, feare.

Therefore drawe neare,

Thou onlie Comforter! with grace

That dothe accorde

Pardon to alle

On Thee that calle

With hope entyre

II. *In Mitten der Krankheit.*
Trœst, herr gott, trœst!
Die krankheit wachst,
Wee und angst fasst
Min seel und lyb.
Darum dich schyb
Gen mir, einiger trost, mit gnad;
Die gwüss erlœst
Ein ieden der
Sin herzlich bger
Und hoffnung setzt
In dich, verschätzt

And strong desyre,

And count erthe's gaine or losse but base.

Nowe alle is o'er!

I noe worde more

Can speake; my tonge is dombe,

My senses all are nombe.

Forthy, 'tis neede

That Thou do pleade

My cause at lengthe.

I have no strengthe

Wherewyth I mighte

  Darzuo diss zyts all nutz und schad.
  Nun ist es um.
  Min zung ist stumm,
  Mag sprechen nit ein wort.
  Min sinn sind all verdorrt.
  Darum ist zyt
  Dass du min stryt
  Fuerist fürhin,
  So ich nit bin
  So stark, dass ich
  Mœg tapferlich

A GODLIE HYMNE.

Fyght the goode fighte,
And bolde withstonde
The Divell's wyles and cruell honde.
Yet fixt shall be,
Howe'er he rage, my hearte on Thee!

III. *Whenne hys sicknesse was amended.*

Helthe, helthe, O Lorde!
I thynke at laste
The paryl paste,
Thou willynge, sinne

Thuon widerstand
Des tüfels facht und frefner hand.
Doch wirt min gmuet
Stæt blyben dir, wie er joch wuet.

III. *In der Besserung.*

Gsund, herr gott, gsund!
Ich mein ich keer
Schon widrum her.
Ja wenn dich dunkt,

Shal ne'er againe

On erthe mee in hys daunger holde.

My mouthe Thy worde

And praise, moche more

Than e'er before,

Shall publyshe wyde

Withouten guile, all plaine and bolde.

Though I must paye

Dethe's debt one daye,

And it indeede may bee

With greater payne to mee

Der sünden funk
Werd nit meer bherschen mich uf erd,
So muoss min mund
Din lob und leer
Ussprechen meer
Dann vormals ic,
Wie es joch geh,
Einfaltiglich on alle gfærd.
Wiewol ich muoss
Des todes buoss
Erlyden zwar einmal

A GODLIE HYMNE.

Than hadde befel,

Lorde, if Thy wille

But even nowe

Hadde bid me goe,

Yet wol I beare

The stryfe and care

Of erthe, O Lorde,

In joyfulle hope of Thy rewarde,

Wyth helpe from Thee,

Withoute whych nought may parfyt bee!

Villycht mit grœssrem qual
Dann iezund wær
Geschehen, herr,
So ich sunst bin
Nach gfaren hin,
So will ich doch
Den trutz und poch
In diser welt
Tragen frœlich um widergelt
Mit hilfe din,
On den nüt mag vollkommen syn.

TO —— ——

Beloved! thou whose tender care hath fed
My flickering lamp of life for many a year,
Thou who hast watched beside my weary bed,
And dried with loving hand the frequent tear,—

Who, when each healing art had proved in vain,
With a strong arm thy helpless burthen bore,
Despite the threatenings of the stormy main,
To milder breezes on a foreign shore,—

Sweet was our rest in Arno's lovely vale,
Amid her olive groves, her orange bowers,
And if health came not on the balmy gale,
Better than health the memory of such hours!

Nor less delight from Elmo's rock to gaze
On the proud city spread so fair below,
And on that classic sea red with the rays
Of such a sunset as those skies may show.

What awful pleasure, too, at midnight stirred,
When from Vesuvius, like a sudden day,
Shot the wild flames and molten lava poured,
Turning to blood the waters of that bay!

Lifting my languid head, thou bad'st me look
Where blazing rocks in showers were upward driven,
With mighty thunderings from below, that shook
As if the fiends of hell again made war on heaven.

And all one golden winter did we lie
Rocked softly on the breast of Nilus old,
Silent with wonder, as we floated by
Pharaonic glories still left half untold.

Beneath the shadow of Arabian palms
Thou'st gently fanned my heavy eyes to rest,
Praying new life might come with spicy balms
Breathed o'er me from the land well named 'the Blest.'

On hallowed Olivet our feet have trod,
Where He of Nazareth was wont to pray,—
We wept o'er Salem that disowned her God,
Her glorious garments stained, her kingdom rent away.

Fair was our summer home as childhood's dream,
Where, robed in clouds of canvas floating free,—
While gilded barges gay his bosom gem—
The dark blue Bosphorus hastes from sea to sea.

Greece, with her purple islands swathed in gold,
Her skies transparent as the Ægean flood,
Her mountains that heaven's rainbow-robes enfold—
Even on that mythic shore together we have stood.

TO —— ——.

Nor sight of Nature's fairest scenes alone
I owe thy love, O friend most true and wise!
Art's highest wonders, old and new, thou'st shown,
And taught me how to see, and how to prize.

And thy beloved voice hath charmed mine ear
With many a sage's, many a nation's lore,
Lifting my soul above each selfish care,
When on the page sublime these eyes could look no
    more.

Lo, now the humble offering that I make!—
A poor return for culture—well I know!—
Given with such liberal hand—yet do thou take!—
And may some future day fruits less unworthy show!

THE END.

www.ingramcontent.com/pod-product-compliance
Lightning Source LLC
Chambersburg PA
CBHW030751230426
43667CB00007B/928